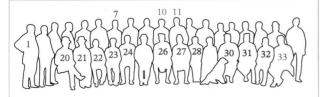

1. W. Hart
7. George Gear
10. George Shorter
11. Arthur Atkins
20. John Longden?
21. George Warren

22. Oscar Ferry
23. T. Smith
24. Richard Hyem
26. James Brown?
27. James Campbell
28. Stephen Maslin

30. Francis Clarke?
31. Alexander Rankin?
32. John Seymour
33. Charlie Thomson?

ROYAL SERVICE

VOLUME III

ROYAL SERVICE

VOLUME III

David Stanley
with
Henry Pownall
and John Tamplin

THIRD MILLENNIUM PUBLISHING
IN ASSOCIATION WITH
VICTORIAN PUBLISHING

Published by Third Millennium Publishing
in association with Victorian Publishing
Copyright © David Stanley 2001

The moral right of David Stanley to be identified as the
author of this work has been asserted in accordance
with the Copyright, Designs and Patents Acts of 1988

A catalogue record for this book is available
from the British Library

ISBN 1 903942 05 5

Designed and produced by
Pardoe Blacker Limited
a member of the Third Millennium Group
Lingfield · Surrey

Printed in China
by Midas Printing

Contents

Photographic credits

Aberdeen City Libraries 15; Authors' Collection 10, 18 (*top*), 19 (*top*), 21 (*top*), 22 (*top*), 28, 30, 31 (*top*), 41 (*top*), 52 (*bottom*), 54 (*top*), 56 (*left*), 57 (*top*), 60, 62; Authors' Collection (A.C. Cooper Ltd) 8, 9, 16, 17 (*top*), 24 (*bottom*), 25 (*middle*); Cyril Dickman, Esq 27; A.F. Flatow Collection 19 (*bottom*), 25 (*bottom*), 59 (*top*); J.B. Hayward, Esq 15 (*bottom*); Maidstone Carriage Museum (the late Mrs Albert Broom) 23 (*bottom*); Noel Morris, Esq 25 (*top*); Royal Collection 12, 31 (*bottom*), 32, 33, 34, 35, 36, 37, 38, 39, 40, 41, (*bottom and right*), 42, 43, 44, 45, 46, 47 (*top left and bottom*), 48, 49 (*right and bottom*), 50, 51, 52 (*top*), 53, 54 (*middle and bottom*), 55, 56 (*right*), 57 (*bottom*), 58, 59; R.J. Scarlett, Esq 17 (*bottom*), 18 (*bottom*), 20, 22 (*left and bottom*), 23 (*top*), 24 (*middle and bottom left*), 26, 47; Sotheby 24 (*top left*); Patrick Street, Esq 49 (*top left*); Mrs G.S.C. Waddington 21 (*bottom*).

Introduction

IN 1996, THE CENTENARY YEAR of the institution of the Royal Victorian Order and the Royal Victorian Medal, Volume I of *Royal Service* was published. It recorded the history of the Order, the Medal and the Royal Victorian Chain and all substantive appointments to the Order and substantive awards of the Medal. It also recorded all holders of the Royal Victorian Chain.

Volume II completes that history, bringing the appointments and awards up to date and recording all honorary appointments to the Order and all honorary awards of the Medal. It also includes the history of the Royal Family Orders, and an account of various medals and badges of office connected with the Royal Households.

This Volume records the history of the Royal Household Long and Faithful Service Medals, together with a register of all recipients.

In 1951, the Order and Medals Research Society had published with the permission of King George VI, a booklet entitled *The Royal Family Orders, Badges of Office, Royal Household Medals and Souvenirs*. It was compiled by G.P.L. James and was limited to three hundred and fifty copies. It was followed in 1954 by a small supplement edited by R.E. Harbord, with the permission of the Queen. Both publications were the first in their field and have long been out of print.

The authors have thought it right to record their debt to those who first researched this field. It is their work which has led directly to the appearance of these three volumes which cover a wider field and in much greater detail.

London, 2001

THE DECORATIONS OF MISS MACDONALD (*left to right*) top row: Special Gold Medal, Member of Royal Victorian Order (subsequently promoted to Lieutenant, 31 December 1985), Royal Victorian Medal; second row: Silver Jubilee Medal 1935, Coronation Medal 1937, Coronation Medal 1953; third row: Silver Jubilee Medal 1977 and The Long and Faithful Service Medal with two bars.

The Long and Faithful
Service Medals

====

OF ALL HONOURS AND AWARDS connected with Royal service, Queen Elizabeth II's Long and Faithful Service Medal could be said to be one of the most exclusive, so precise are the regulations as to who can receive it. The medal is only awarded to Royal staff, both indoor and outdoor, who work in the Royal residences and on the Royal estates. It is given for twenty years service to the Queen, the Duke of Edinburgh or Queen Elizabeth The Queen Mother, and to the late Queen Mary, but not for service to any other member of the Royal family. Bars may be awarded to mark completion of thirty, forty and fifty years service. Staff who are subsequently promoted to officials, who have already received the medal cannot then receive the bars since they are eligible for appointments in the Royal Victorian Order. The Queen likes, where possible, to give the Medal personally. The bars are usually presented by heads of departments, except in the case of such personal staff as the Queen's Dressers and Pages of the Backstairs, when the Queen presents them herself.

Though the medal is normally struck in silver, a special and unique award in gold was given by the Queen on 13 July 1978. The medal (which like the gold Royal Victorian Medal is silver gilt) was presented to Miss Margaret Macdonald who entered Royal service as a nursery maid on 1 September 1926, a few months after the birth of Princess Elizabeth and had completed nearly fifty-two years service. Miss Macdonald had been the Queen's Dresser since 1952 and was in the Queen's service for more than sixty-six years. She died on September 1993, aged 89.

SPECIAL GOLD MEDAL
A silver gilt Long and Faithful Service Medal specially produced by the Royal Mint with the normal ribbon to which two gold stripes were added and woven by the Royal School of Needlework. Presented by the Queen to her Dresser, Miss Margaret Macdonald.

There are many instances of several generations of families serving the Sovereign and receiving the Faithful Service Medals. The past four chief bookbinders to the Royal Library at Windsor Castle are typical examples. Frederick Vaughan, (bookbinder 1873–1914) and his son Frank, (bookbinder 1914–1939) received medals, the former the Victoria Faithful Service Medal, the latter the George V Long and Faithful Service Medal. In the present reign Ernest Day (bookbinder 1939–1976) and his son Richard (bookbinder since 1976) have both been honoured with the Elizabeth II Long and Faithful Service Medal. Ernest Day's award was one of the first of the reign and in 1964 and 1974 he received bars for thirty years and forty years service. His son received his medal in 1976, but his subsequent promotion to official disqualified him from receiving a thirty year bar in 1986 and any subsequent bars in the future. Years of loyal service to the monarch, exemplified by four generations of bookbinders and the devotion of such staff as Miss Macdonald, continue the traditions which prompted the institution of the first Faithful Service Medals in Queen Victoria's reign.

At Balmoral, on her birthday, the 24 May 1872, Queen Victoria made the first presentations of her new Faithful Service Medal. Accounts of this appear in her journal for that day and in a letter written to Prince Arthur:

'After breakfast gave the Victoria Faithful Service Medal to Brown, Loehlein, Heale, Maslin, Searle and Cowley, each coming in singly and expressing in their different ways, their gratification. It [the medal] is just like the gold one [the Devoted Service Medal, already given to Brown, referred to later] and the 3 other Pages [and] Cullen, Taylor P[age] of the Presence etc., are to get it on my return, altogether 14 in this Birthday'.

A GROUP OF FIVE SERVANTS, taken at Balmoral 1872 by George Washington Wilson, the Aberdeen photographer. All were recipients of Queen Victoria's Faithful Service Medal in the year of its institution. (*left to right*) William Cullen, Stephen Maslin, Charles Green, George Searle and (*seated on the ground*) Spencer Cowley.

Henry Ponsonby, the Queen's private secretary, wrote to his wife 'the chief servants were decorated with the medal and walk about highly pleased with them'. No doubt his wife knew as much about the medal as anyone did, for the presentations marked the culmination of eight months work on the project by her husband. So for its beginnings, we must go back to the last quarter of 1871.

In September 1871 Queen Victoria suffered the most serious illness in her life and had been very close to death. This had coincided with a period in her reign when her popularity was at its lowest ebb, due to her continued seclusion and withdrawal from public duties following the death of the Prince Consort. Her ministers and members of her household, alarmed by the situation, were embarking on their most desperate measures yet, to force her out of retirement. As a consequence, with the onset of her illness, it was not taken seriously, everyone thinking that this was the Queen's method of retaliation to the pressure against which she found herself. Only weeks later, when the Queen had not apparently improved and was indeed much worse, did they realise how seriously ill she was. The same reservations, fortunately, were not held by her personal servants who had actually seen her, and attended her devotedly throughout, foremost of these being the ever-faithful John Brown. It seems likely that it was with this in mind, that on her recovery in late September, she turned her attention to some form of reward for these servants and, especially, for Brown. On 2 October 1871 the Queen wrote to her Prime Minister, Mr Gladstone:

'There is a subject wh the Queen wld have mentioned to Mr Gladstone yesterday but that she felt she was unequal to talk much – She therefore writes it. – It is one wh she has often thought of of late – & wh she thinks will strike Mr Gladstone as well worth entertaining. It is not yet in a form to be discussed in detail – but the Queen hopes vy shortly to be able to send it him in such a form as to be capable of serious consideration.

It is the subject of some distinctive badge or honour of a lower grade wh in the line the Queen wld propose does not exist in England tho' does abroad. There are medals given to Arctic discoverers – including officers and men; – also of late for saving life at sea &c. – Non-commissioned officers receive Good Conduct Medals – as well as for bravery in the field. –

Now there are services, in their way equally valuable meritorious & indeed important & those are: personal, devoted & faithful services to the Sovereign, wh pass by without any distinctive badge wh wld be an object of pride & gratitude & emulation to many – who feel that they have done as much & far more as many gentlemen at Court – & yet no one ever hears of them. What in fact can be more important than the faithfulness & discretion & independant unselfishness of those personal servants who are constantly about the Sovereign, who, as everyone is, must in many ways be vy dependent on them ?– To encourage & rward them independent of money wld be to raise them in their own eyes & those of the Public. – Now in Prussia & Grandducal Hesse – the small medal to be worn at the button hole, is given to the Servants who have served 25 & 50 years; for long or particularly faithful Servants – with the Sovereign's head on one side & the person's name & any remark as to the peculiar service wh entitles them to it.– This has struck the Queen as an excellent plan. It wld merely require a small sum to furnish the Medals – wh the Queen thinks the Treasury wld easily grant. It wld give these people the feeling that the humblest services are prized & recognised – & not for ever un-noticed, on acct of these humbler positions, while gentlemen may look to Orders &c. In these days especially the Queen thinks it wld have a vy good effect.'

Gladstone having no ideas of his own on the subject discussed the matter with the Queen's Private Secretary. Ponsonby had the idea of extending the award of the Army Long Service Medal, but the Prime Minister was not in agreement. Ponsonby then mentioned the Ladies' Order of Victoria and Albert. This Gladstone grasped enthusiastically and suggested extending it to include a fourth class for everyone.

On 3 October he replied to the Queen's note putting forward the idea of enlarging the Order of Victoria and Albert, though adding tactfully that he 'would not advise an application to the House of Commons on the subject and thinks that among other points, it would be inconvenient as tending towards interference with Your Majesty's discretion in the grant of the distinction. But he thinks there would be no difficulty in meeting the small expense entailed.'

The fact that Brown was to be the principal recipient of the proposed award was certain to provoke opposition from the Queen's family. The Queen had already mentioned her idea to Princess Alice. Ponsonby recounts a subsequent conversation he had with the Princess on the matter, in a letter to his wife.

A GROUP OF QUEEN VICTORIA'S FOOTMEN, Balmoral *c.*1870 (*left to right*) William Power, Ed... Beale, Charlie Thomson, Thomas Newell, Edward Collins, William Kiddle, Ed... Jackson and William Henry Blake

Princess Alice – 'then what an unfortunate idea this is of hers about the decoration.' 'Well M'am I don't see that,' Ponsonby replied, 'I think a medal may be as well bestowed for long and faithful personal service to the Queen, as for similar services performed by soldiers and non-commissioned officers who may have never been in war, but have been excellent servants in peace. Besides they have some such order in Prussia and I thought you had in Darmstadt?.' 'Yes, of course we have and an excellent thing it is, if properly bestowed, but with us it is governed by as strict regulations as your military medal is, given only to those who have served 25 or 50 years well and fully. But here it is intended to make two classes, the first of which is to be given

quite irrespective of time and probably to only one person, the second governed by certain rules which may or may not be adhered to – however I am getting our rules from Darmstadt for the Queen to see.'

Though Ponsonby defended the Queen's proposals to the Princess, he expressed his doubts on another aspect of the scheme in a letter two days later: 'I foresee troubles' he confided to his wife,

'if she [the Queen] gives it to Brown and Loehlein – well and good. But if she gives it to the keepers and gillies here [at Balmoral] the English will be angry and she will give it purely herself. I fear that favouritism will crop through fearfully.'

This early atmosphere of opposition from those around her seems to account for the rather uncharacteristically defensive tone of the Queen's letter to her Prime Minister. On 12 October, in a long and rather confused note to Ponsonby, the Queen, now armed with the rules and regulations of the Hessian service medal, attempted to set out her proposals for the new award and asked her Private Secretary to make a draft summary. Though she was to change her mind frequently over the smaller details, her basic proposals, set out in this note, were to remain largely the same. These were that the medal, to be called the 'Victoria Faithful Service Medal', should bear on one side her effigy. On the reverse was to be engraved the name of the recipient. Medals would be in both gold and silver. Awards would generally be made for length of service, but they could also be given for specially meritorious services, irrespective of length. It would only be given to her personal servants, those with whom she came into day to day contact. Ponsonby made the draft and put it up to the Queen. During the next few weeks little progress seems to have been made, and he confided to his wife that he had 'had more interviews on the subject of the medal which is getting too difficult for me'. Perhaps sensing her Private Secretary's frustration, the Queen did not refer to the matter again for nearly three months, while holding on to the draft which she showed to Arthur Helps (the editor of *Leaves from the Journal of Our Life in the Highlands*) 'who highly approved of it and the way in which it was drawn out' and to Sir Thomas Biddulph (Keeper of the Privy Purse) and whom she asked to discuss with Ponsonby a suitable ribbon.

On 24 January 1872, Ponsonby received another long note. In this the Queen largely repeated, but expanded slightly on, her earlier proposals, asking him if he could condense parts of the original draft. This painfully slow process might have continued as indecisively as ever, but for an incident which occurred on 29 February. On that date, an unsuccessful attempt was made on the Queen's life, from which John Brown, at any rate in his monarch's eyes, emerged as the hero of the hour. But for the gillie's presence of mind, she might have been dead. This was the sixth attempt on the Queen's life during her reign though, as it transpired, she had not on this occasion been in any particular danger. At the garden entrance of Buckingham Palace, a simple-minded youth, Arthur O'Connor, pointed an unloaded and defective flintlock (which was later found to have been stuffed with wads of paper and leather) at the Queen as she was about to get out of her carriage. His plan had been merely to frighten her, and force her into ordering the release of Fenian prisoners. Brown had first pushed O'Connor aside and, when the boy had run around to the side of the carriage, he had held him by the scruff of the neck, assisted by Fleming, the Queen's Page, and Clark, a footman, until the police took him in charge. Fleming was to comment in his diary that the Queen had remained perfectly calm, standing up in the carriage until O'Connor was taken away. Her own account of the incident in her journal was somewhat different. 'I was trembling vy much and a sort of shiver ran through me. It is to good Brown and to his wonderful presence of mind I greatly owe my safety, for he alone saw the boy rush round and followed him!' Prince Arthur had in fact tried to jump over the carriage to reach him too, but was too slow. The Prince of Wales, later, was to complain that his brother had acted just as gallantly as the highlander but had received nothing other than a gold pin. Instant recognition was now required for Brown's devotion, in the form of her new medal.

On 5 March the Queen wrote to Ponsonby; 'The Queen told good Brown in a note today, she gave him, of her intention. He received it with his usual simplicity – but was greatly pleased – & when the Queen said it would be put in the papers – he said it was too kind and more than he deserved.........the Queen is sorry that the medal can't be ready before two months.' Meanwhile the Queen presented the highlander with a gold watch.

Ponsonby had, in fact, contacted Mr Wyon who, he informed the Queen, was already coming down to Windsor with his sketches, in two days time, at one o'clock on 7th March. After this meeting, Ponsonby made a summary for the Queen of his discussion with the medallist.

Wyon was anxious about the length of the inscriptions to be engraved on both the gold and silver medals. They should be as brief as possible or the words would have to be so small as to be almost impossible to read. For the gold medal he suggested the following: TO/ MR JOHN BROWN/ IN RECOGNI-TION OF HIS PRESENCE/ OF MIND AND DEVOTION AT/ BUCKINGHAM PALACE/ 29TH FEBRUARY, 1872. This the Queen approved, but for one small alteration. Brown was not to be 'Mr' but 'Esq.' as were Loehlein and all the Pages and other upper servants, who were to receive the silver medals. Wyon proposed engraving on the silver medals the name 'Victoria Faithful Service Medal 1872' around the rim, rather than on the reverse, in order to save space. This was approved.

He calculated at this stage the cost of the die at about £60, which prompted the question from the Queen – 'the die, once made – what would be the cost of the medals?'

On 12 March Wyon was able to send his drawing of the gold medal and a more accurate estimate of the costs: 'The price of the medals and mounts (supposing the dies be purchased for Fifty Guineas) would be as nearly as we could estimate beforehand, as follows:

> Gold, including engraving inscription and case £9-0-0.
> Silver,......................do.............................£3-10-0.

A problem seems to have arisen and various means were put forward, as to the best method of fastening the medals to the recipients' coats. In a letter to Ponsonby on 22 March, Wyon recommended 'a bar brooch from which the medals would be suspended'. He continued, 'It occurs to me that in those cases in which Her Majesty may desire to mark the length of service that Roman numerals indicating such a period might be placed upon the bar'.

Ponsonby agreed with the idea of the brooch bar, but with no numeral, in the first instance when the medal was awarded. He wondered, however, if the

(*left*) JOHN BROWN and (*below*) THE WATCH presented to John Brown by Queen Victoria on the 23 February 1872.

Roman numeral 'X' that the medallist had proposed might be added later in recognition of a further ten years service. Later in the month he wrote again to Wyon, 'On further reflection, that Arabic rather than Roman numerals be used, as the meaning of 'X' and 'XX' on the bar might not be immediately apparent.' In the event no more attention was paid to the subject of bars for further service until the need arose in 1882.

On 17 April, work on the silver medals was sufficiently advanced for Wyon to ask for the full inscriptions to be given to him so that the medals could be engraved. Was the same title, he asked, which had been previously agreed for the rims of these medals to be put on the gold? The gold medal, he was informed, was to have a different inscription. This was to be 'Victoria Devoted Service Medal 1872'.

THE DEVOTED SERVICE
MEDAL awarded to John
Brown in 1872.

Wyon, therefore, signified his intention of engraving the rim of the one gold medal and to incorporate that on the silver medals, as part of the die, the letters of which would appear in relief. However, the length of the inscriptions the Queen required to be engraved on the reverse of the silver medals, still proved a problem. She was very loath to alter them in any way and suggested at this late stage that the actual medals be made larger, somehow using the same dies. Patiently Wyon replied that this could not be done, but suggested in turn that more space might be gained by removing the wreaths from the reverses of the medals. The final compromise solution came from the Queen. The former inscription previously agreed for the rims of the medals was to be discarded and replaced by part of the inscription which was to be included on the reverses. Around the rims were now to be the following words: 'Presented by Queen Victoria 1872'. As this wording was part of the die, medals awarded in later years continued to bear the date of institution on the rim. The actual year of award was engraved on the reverse under the inscription; those given in 1872 have no date engraved on them.

On 7 May a delighted Sovereign wrote to her Private Secretary. 'The Queen has just given the medal to good Brown who is very much pleased with it, greatly admires it and is very grateful and for all the trouble Colonel Ponsonby has taken.' In *The Times* appeared the following announcement:

'The Queen, who had contemplated instituting a medal for long and faithful service amongst Her Majesty's domestic servants, has inaugurated the institution by conferring on Mr John Brown, the Queen's personal attendant, a medal in gold, with an annuity of £25 attached to it, as a mark of her appreciation of his presence of mind and of his devotion on the occasion of the attack made upon Her Majesty in Buckingham Palace Gardens on 29th February, 1872.'

The pleasure of seeing her favourite gillie wearing his new award seems to have diverted the Queen's mind from the silver medals for the moment. However on 19 May she wrote to Ponsonby:

'Have the silver medals arrived? the Queen thought they were promised for the 15th. She hopes the joining on to the VR will be strong enough. Brown says he fears that in the gold one it will not stand much wearing or shaking well. In fact the Queen thinks now the medals ought to have been a little larger. The inscription is barely legible to the naked eye – except very strong ones – should this be found to be the case – as there are not likely to be many, some day they could be replaced by precisely the same pattern only larger and more substantial.'

The Queen commanded that booklets be printed containing the rules and regulations, lists of recipients and colour plates illustrating the gold and silver medals and their respective ribbons. The Queen's copy was bound in Royal Stewart tartan, the same as the ribbon. Other copies, to be kept in the Privy Purse and other offices for reference, were bound in blue and gold. It was later decided that medal recipients should each receive a booklet and these were issued with plain blue card covers. The 1872 booklets give, in three columns, the name of the recipient, the date and place of presentation and the inscription engraved on the reverse of each medal. It was intended that all booklets should be updated each year with the issue of printed supplements containing new recipients' names and details. When a complete reprint of the booklets was undertaken in April 1882 it was decided not to include the actual day and place of presentation of the medal against the recipients' name but only the year. Under the names of those who had qualified for bars to their medals were added the words 'One bar for service'. Those servants who, by then, were deceased had their names entered in italics and a note of their date of death. It is interesting to see that John Brown's name was not put into italics until some years after his death, during which time several new editions of the booklets were produced. The last of the booklets was printed in 1900.

The Royal Stewart tartan medal ribbon must rank as one of the most elaborate ever manufactured. Unfortunately, there is no reference to its choice or when indeed it was decided to have a medal ribbon at all, for in a letter written on 13 March 1872 to the Empress Frederick, the Queen gives a description of her new medal and continues, 'Instead of a ribbon and to make it unlike military medals there will be a VR surmounted with a crown, and in the same metal as the medal'. Although it seems certain that all the medals, at the time of the first presentations, had ribbons, at what point it was decided they should have them, is not clear. Also, the booklets contain colour plates of two ribbons. Alongside the illustration of the standard ribbon is another, identical but with the addition of small strips of gold lace appliqué down both edges. According to the caption, this is the Devoted Service Medal ribbon. Careful study of photographs of Brown wearing his Devoted Service Medal, clearly shows it being worn from the ordinary Faithful Service Medal ribbon with no such embellishment. The medals loaned for the colour photographs both have the ordinary Faithful Service Medal ribbon.

The yearly selection of recipients seems to have continued quite smoothly for the next ten years. In the first and second years the Queen had ample candidates of her own whom she knew and wished to reward. These, it will be seen, consisted mainly of her indoor staff in 1872 and outdoor staff in 1873. Thereafter she relied largely on a list of long serving staff compiled by her Private Secretary. However, as it transpired, length of service was not of prime importance and in itself no guarantee of being awarded the medal. Two extremes in the number of years of service are to be found in the cases of Joseph Julius Kanne, obviously a particular favourite who received his medal in 1874 after only 14 years, and John Martin who seems to have passed quite unnoticed until 1886 when he received the medal having served 55 years. He subsequently went on to receive a bar in 1896 and was still serving in the Household in a part-time capacity as a Groom of the Great Chamber in 1902, when he received Edward VII's Coronation Medal.

Another very long serving group of servants were the Marshalmen. This body of men whose origins dated back to the reign of Henry VIII, were effectively the Royal Household Police force, then under Officers of the Knight Marshal. By 1897, long after the abolition of the post of Knight Marshal, there were six Marshalmen whose duties were ushers and doormen at Court Functions and at the House of Lords.

In May 1881 Mr David Bennett, one of the Queen's Marshalmen, wrote to Ponsonby drawing the private secretary's attention to his and two of his colleagues' length of service and asking that they be considered for medals. Bennett had entered service in 1837 and completed 43 years service, 27 in the stewards' room and 16 as a Marshalman; Isaac Rayner had been porter in the Clerk of the Kitchens Office for 25 years and a Marshalman for 13. Bennett

THE VICTORIA FAITHFUL SERVICE MEDAL awarded to John Brown in 1872.

VICTORIA FAITHFUL SERVICE MEDALS, (*above*) the reverse for shortest service and (*below*) for longest service

THE QUEEN'S
MARSHALMEN, 1896.

VICTORIA FAITHFUL
SERVICE MEDALS,
obverse and reverse
and bar.

received his medal in 1882 having completed 45 years service but Rayner had to wait until 1893 by which time he had completed 52 years.

In 1882 those recipients who had received medals in the year of institution and were still in service, became eligible for bars, as provided for in the rules.

On 4 January Ponsonby wrote to Wyon asking if a 'bar or clasp can be attached to the Faithful Service Medal bearing on it the figure 10 – and if so how this should be added.... it would probably be necessary to send these medals to Messrs. Wyon for the addition. What would the cost of the new bar be?' The medallist replied that brooch pins would have to be removed and new cases for the medals supplied and that providing there would be no more than 25 medals, in the first instance, to be dealt with, the cost would be no more than £1 per medal, including case. It was ascertained that nine of the original fourteen recipients were eligible for bars and these could be fitted in three weeks.

We may presume that these nine servants were happy with their medals when returned to them by Wyon, with fresh ribbons and new boxes, as were those servants awarded bars in the following year. However, in 1884 two recipients were very unhappy and one sent his box back to Wyon. On 25 June 1884, Alan Wyon, somewhat puzzled, wrote to Ponsonby asking why the case for Mr Gibb's medal had been returned. A note from Henry Ponsonby to his clerk gives the answer. 'please tell him [Wyon] that Hudson and the others don't like the new cases – prefer the old original case as it was given them by the Queen – if he has not destroyed the old case and old piece of ribbon can he send them to the servants?' Wyon managed to recover two boxes and ribbons which were returned.

Five awards of the Victoria Faithful Service Medal were made to the Queen's Indian Attendants between 1889 and 1900. The Queen's decision to present the first of these appears to have been made quite suddenly. However, it is quite possible she had the idea in mind earlier in the year, when in April she ordered that a new proviso be included in the rules and regulations: 'In special cases the medal may be conferred for faithful service irrespective of length'.

The medal had to be struck and engraved in a very short time as the recipient was about to return to India. On Wednesday, 7 August 1889, Ponsonby telegraphed from Osborne to Gibson (Secretary to the Privy Purse) in London, 'I want a Faithful Service Medal complete, as soon as possible, not later than Tuesday next. Tell Wyon to get one ready immediately'. Gibson replied on the following day that 'Wyon can get the medal made in time if he gets the inscription by tonight'.

The medal was to be engraved: PRESENTED BY THE QUEEN EMPRESS VICTORIA TO MUHAMMAD BAKHSH IN RECOGNITION OF HIS FAITHFUL SERVICES TO H.M. AUG: 1889.

On the following Tuesday (13th) a thankful Ponsonby telegraphed Gibson, in London, that the medal had 'just arrived as the Queen sent to ask for it!'

It has already been mentioned that the length of service was irrelevant in terms of qualifying for the medal and it will be noted that in the inscription on Bakhsh's (and on all subsequent awards to the Indian Attendants) no specific number of years' service is mentioned. The average length of service of the Indian servants was in fact only three years. Two of these who had the Faithful Service Medal achieved the added distinction of being awarded the Royal Victorian Medal. Surprisingly the Munshi Abdul Karim was not a Faithful Service Medal recipient. However, he was to achieve greater distinctions, being awarded the CIE (25 May 1895) and the CVO (24 May 1899).

QUEEN VICTORIA'S INDIAN ATTENDANTS' DECORATION. Examples are known of this decoration, but no information has been found about it. The Munshi wears it in the photograph below.

THE MUNSHI, Queen Victoria's Indian Secretary, Abdul Karim, c.1895, a notable non-recipient of the Victorian Faithful Service Medal. He is wearing, on the top row, the Companion of the Order of the Indian Empire, Order of the Red Eagle (Prussia), Order of Philip, Knight, 2nd class (Hesse) and the House Order of Saxe-Coburg; on the bottom row, General Medal of Honour (Hesse) and the Indian Attendant's Decoration.

He may also have been the only recipient of what has been supposed to be Queen Victoria's Indian Attendants' Decoration. In the Royal Archives there is a note from the Queen dated October 27th 1890, at Balmoral 'The Queen has presented the Munshi with the decoration of an Eastern Star. (signed) VRI,' which may refer to this. Several examples of this award have been seen, but its origins and use are obscure.

Only three awards of the Faithful Service Medal were given to women. These were not mounted on bows, as might be expected, but ribboned exactly the same as the medals given to the men.

In July 1885, Princess Beatrice, the youngest of the Queen's children, married Prince Henry of Battenburg at Whippingham Parish Church near Osborne House. In 1895 the Prince obtained for himself the post of Military Secretary to the commander, Major-General Sir Francis Scott who was leading an expedition to West Africa to put an end to King Prempeh of Kumasi's raids on the Gold Coast for slaves which, in spite of an ultimatum from the British Government, had continued. Arriving safely at the Cape Coast, the expedition set out on 27 December 1895 to march to Kumasi. On 10 January 1896 Prince Henry was struck down with malaria and in spite of all the efforts of his doctors and the devotion of his servant, Butcher, he died ten days later. His body was brought back to Portsmouth in HMS *Blenheim* and two days later, on 3 February, was buried at Whippingham.

On 11 February Sir Fleetwood Edwards wrote to Walter Gibson in London:

> 'The Queen wants to give George Butcher (Prince Henry's Valet) a medal – it is to be exactly like the Faithful Service Medal in silver – but will have a different inscription at the back and a different ribbon. Will you therefore order one and I will send you the inscription for the reverse later.'

The information was passed to Alan Wyon, who informed Gibson on the 12th that the medal had been put in hand and that he presumed that the silver pendant was to be the same as that on an ordinary Faithful Service Medal. The medal would be ready for engraving in two or three days. Some difficulty seems to have been encountered in finding a suitable ribbon. Though it was intended that the colour should be red with white edge stripes, after a great deal of correspondence with Messrs Redmaynes who were to supply the ribbon, the medal, when presented, had the standard Faithful Service Medal ribbon attached to it. The medal was to be engraved both on the rim and on the reverse. Around the rim was the insription: PRESENTED BY VICTORIA R.I. FEB: 1896 and on the reverse, within the wreath: TO GEORGE BUTCHER VALET TO H.R.H. PRINCE HENRY OF BATTENBURG IN RECOGNITION OF HIS DEVOTED AND FAITHFUL SERVICES TO HIS DEAR MASTER.

Butcher was retained by Princess Beatrice and became her Steward. He was given the Royal Victorian Medal (silver) by Edward VII in 1904.

In May 1892 occurred the first instance of a recipient becoming eligible for a second bar to his medal. This was George Searle, one of the Queen's Pages of the Backstairs who had entered the service of Princess Augusta in 1836 and the Queen's in 1842. In 1892 he completed 50 years in the Royal household, and had been one of the first recipients of the medal in its year of institution. It is recorded that his medal was returned to Wyon, for a second bar to be fitted, on 20 May 1892. Whether or not this bar bore the number

VICTORIA FAITHFUL SERVICE MEDAL: obverse with two bars.

QUEEN VICTORIA'S
SERVANTS in the South
of France, probably
Grasse, 1891.

'20', as provided for in the rules and regulations is not clear, but it seems
unlikely as three other two-bar medals that have been seen by the author
were all fitted with two 10-year bars.

After the death of Queen Victoria in 22nd January 1901, no more awards
of the Victoria Faithful Service Medal were made, nor were any bars given.

In Edward VII's short reign, no consideration seems to have been given by
him to the creation of a Long Service Medal for his servants. Even the Royal
Victorian Medal, which he bestowed quite liberally everywhere else, was
given to very few of his own servants.

King George V did, however, consider the matter and instituted the George
V Long and Faithful Service Medal in 1913. The first awards were made in
May of that year. This was the 20th anniversary of his marriage to Princess
Mary of Teck and of his setting up of an independant household of his own.
Those servants who had been in his or his wife's service – first as Duke
and Duchess of York and later as Duke and Duchess of Cornwall and
York, then Prince and Princess of Wales and finally as King and
Queen – who had completed 20 years, were eligible for the new
medal. Eleven servants received the medal in 1913 and a total of 66
awards were made in the years 1913–1929. Those servants of
Queen Victoria and Edward VII who were retained by George V
at his accession and who in many cases had already completed
more than 20 years service under one or both of these monarchs,
had to do a full 20 years with George V to qualify. Thus, in 1930,
no less than 264 servants qualified for the medal, the greatest
number in any year of the reign.

In general, the requirement to qualify for the medal was 20 years
continuous service. An interesting exception is that of Sidney John
Miller, George V's Second Valet. Having entered the King's (or, as
he was then, the Prince of Wales's) service as a Brusher in 1902, Miller
decided, early in 1910, that he would quit Royal service to try his hand at
ranching in Canada in partnership with a friend. The Prince was very

SIDNEY JOHN MILLER,
Second Valet to King
George V, as a cowboy
in Canada, after he quit
Royal Service, c.1910.

SIDNEY JOHN
MILLER'S MEDALS,
including the Royal
Victorian Medal and the
George V Long and
Faithful Service Medal
with a thirty-year bar.

GEORGE V LONG AND
FAITHFUL SERVICE
MEDALS, obverse and
reverse of 1st type and
the 1st type bars.

(right) GEORGE V
LONG AND FAITHFUL
SERVICE TOKENS,
obverse and reverse.

reluctant to lose him and made Miller promise that he would return if things did not work out. In the event Miller left in January 1910 and returned in the following July. During Miller's absence Edward VII had died and the Prince was now King. Miller was taken back into Royal service from 1 August 1910 as Second Valet to His Majesty.

If Miller's service had been continuous he would have received his medal in July 1922, but as he had been out of service January to August 1910, he received his medal in January 1923. Thus his medal is unusual in that it is engraved 1902–1923.

The medals, like the Victoria Faithful Service Medals, were smaller than war medals. They bore on the obverse the King's uncrowned effigy with the usual legend and on the reverse, in relief, surrounded by a wreath of laurel, the words FOR LONG AND FAITHFUL SERVICE. This reverse was designed by W.H.J. Blackmore, an engraver employed at the Royal Mint. The recipient's name was engraved around the rim. On those medals awarded between 1913 and 1929 the recipient's full name is given in capitals, e.g. ALBERT EDWARD WAKEFORD. On those medals given in 1930 only the recipient's surname appears, preceded by one initial, e.g. G. SCOTT. Engraved on the narrow suspension bar were the dates of the recipient's service, either side of the King's crowned cypher, e.g. 1893–1913, 1902–1922. It was anticipated that some recipients would become eligible for bars and the first of these were awarded in 1923. They took the form of scrolls on which, in relief, appear the words THIRTY YEARS. The bars were attached by means of spikes, soldered on to the reverse, which were pushed through the medal ribbon and bent over at the back. Bars of similar design were produced with the words FORTY YEARS.

In 1931 instructions were given to the Royal Mint to re-design the suspenders of the medals. These had proved to be too delicate and were liable to bend and even break. The suspender was, therefore, strengthened and the G.V.R. cypher incorporated on the reverse as well as on the obverse. It was also widened by one-eighth of an inch.

Attention was also given to the bars which were completely redesigned. For the sake of uniformity those recipients with the 'scroll type' thirty-year bars were, if they became eligible for them, given 'scroll type' forty-year bars.

With the introduction of the 2nd type medals the style of naming seems to have been altered, though it is not consistent. The surname was

GEORGE V LONG AND
FAITHFUL SERVICE
MEDALS, 2nd type bars.

now given first, in capitals followed by the recipient's first christian name, in upper and lower case, followed by one other initial, e.g. HOOKS, Robert H.

In 1930, small badges, intended to be worn suspended from a watch chain and known as Royal Household Long Service Tokens, were first given to workers on the Royal Estates who had completed 20 years service. These were given instead of medals. Subsequently many recipients exchanged these Tokens for Long and Faithful Service Medals.

In the short reign of Edward VIII no Long and Faithful Service Medals bearing his effigy and cypher were awarded. Though an obverse die to serve both the Royal Victorian Medal and the Long and Faithful Service Medal was prepared by the Mint and finished on 2 November 1936 and a batch of twelve Royal Victorian Medals were struck, apart from a specimen in the Mint Museum there is no record of any Long and Faithful Service Medals being supplied. It is interesting to note that the cypher mount to the medal in the Mint Museum is completely different to Edward VIII's standard cypher and is an adaptation of George V's cypher. Problems were encountered in using the standard cypher as will be explained later.

During the reign, however, twenty-one George V pattern Long and Faithful Service Medals were awarded. Four were ordered from the Royal Mint on the 21 February 1936 and the remainder on 9 July.

GEORGE V LONG AND
FAITHFUL SERVICE
MEDALS, obverse and
reverse of 2nd type.

ROYAL MEWS, BUCKINGHAM PALACE, 1930. Some of the staff who were awarded the George V Long and Faithful Service Medal, having completed 20 years service, photographed together with the Master of the Horse and the Crown Equerry. From left, top row: J. Norman, *Carriage Painter*; E. Pugh, *Groom*; L. Dickinson, *Groom*; W. Taylor, *Driver*; F. McIlveen, *Gate Porter*; M. Newman, *Driver*; G. Shiner, *Postillion*; F. Sanders, *Stable Helper*; A. Bunce, *Driver*; E. Price, *Carriage Washer*; S. West, *Postillion*; J. Game, *Groom*; R. Parr, *Postillion*.
Middle row: E. Rapley, *Storeman*; J. Cooper, *Carriage Washer*; W. Francis, *Stud Helper*; E. Pellett, *Stud Helper*; J. Halse, *Stud Helper*; W. Moores, *Harness Cleaner*; J. Clarke, *Postillion*; P. Simmonds, *Postillion*; W. Bacon, *Groom*; J. Slack, *Postillion*; R. Land, *Postillion*; A. Minter, *Carriage Washer*; W. Murking, *Postillion*; W. Wraight, *Carriage Washer*; E. Fisher, *Postillion*; T.E. Champion, *Postillion*.
Front row, seated: A. Howard, *Driver*; J. Hardy, *Gate Porter*; A. Pryor, *Coachman*; Sir A. Erskine, *Crown Equerry*; Earl of Granard, *Master of the Horse*; E. Lines, *Coachman*; F. Baker, *Coachman*; A. O'Mara, *Coachman*.

EDWARD VIII LONG
AND FAITHFUL
SERVICE MEDAL, (top)
the rejected design for
the obverse and (below)
the final obverse and
reverse. This medal was
struck but not issued. It
is in the collection of the
Royal Mint. No ribbon
was woven.

The first batch were for servants whose medals were due and whose names were under consideration at the time of George V's death. The second batch were awards to senior servants whose eligibility had apparently been overlooked. Just over half of these should apparently have received medals in 1930. Whereas those 264 servants who were given their medals in 1930 received the 1st type medals, these late awards were of the 2nd type. Since all the medals were given in recognition of service to the late King, it was thought appropriate that they should be George V medals. Also as the regulations stood, to qualify for the medal all service had to be to the same monarch.

Though George VI acceded on 12 December 1936, his Long and Faithful Service Medal was not instituted until almost eight years into the reign.

On 25 August 1943, the Keeper of the Privy Purse, Sir Ulick Alexander, wrote to the Deputy Master of the Mint, J.H. McC. Craig, on the subject of 'a Long and Faithful Service Medal for Household servants and it is His Majesty's wish that the medal should be the same as King George V's Long and Faithful Service Medal with the exception that it would bear H.M.'s effigy and cypher and could arrangements be made for this new medal to be struck as soon as it is conveniently possible, as it is The King's intention to grant a number of them at the same time as the [1944] New Year Honours list is published'.

Craig replied on 27 August 1943, that there would be no difficulty in producing the new Household Service Medals by the end of the year. 'But some modification of His Majesty's standard cypher, or its surround would be necessary' and he ventured to ask whether 'the King would be willing to approve the use of an adaptation of King George V's cypher? As the outside line of the cypher defined the design and the cypher was used on both the obverse and the reverse, the outside curve of the G and the outside curves of the R must be identical. Each letter also had to have a fairly thick tail for rivetting to the disc part of the medal'.

OFFICIAL CYPHERS of George V, Edward VIII and George VI.

A drawing was submitted with the proposed arrangement, together with a specimen of a 2nd type George V medal.

This difficulty had been encountered already with Edward VIII's cypher and becomes readily apparent when his and his brother George VI's are compared with their father's, George V's.

A month later Alexander wrote to Craig to say that the King had appreciated the difficulty of using his standard cypher and had approved the modification.

THE MEDALS of
Ephraim James
Rainbow MVO.

THE MEDALS OF JOHN POTTINGER, Yeoman of the Cellars, one of the two recipients of George VI's Royal Victorian Medal in gold and only the second man to achieve the distinction of a fifty-year bar to his Long and Faithful Service Medal. The medal had been awarded in 1913.

Similar approval must have been obtained from Edward VIII for the adaptation of his cypher as is evident from the specimen of his Long and Faithful Service Medal, already mentioned, in the Royal Mint Museum.

A striking of the new Royal Household Medal was submitted to the King on 23 November 1943. Meanwhile, on 12 November 1943, the Royal Warrant had been published establishing the new medal. The rules were now changed. Servants with George VI prior to his accession, could count that period of service towards the 20 years required to qualify. Servants who had served King George V and/or King Edward VIII could now count that service and those with George V medals could qualify for bars to their medals.

Thus two of George V's servants, still in service, who had received the King's medal in 1913, its year of institution, qualified for fifty-year bars. The first of these was George Pottinger, one of the King's Pages of the Presence, who received his bar on 1 February 1943. Pottinger achieved the added distinction of being one of the only two gold Royal Victorian Medal recipients of George VI's reign. He was followed by David Allan, Tapissier to Queen Mary at Marlborough House, who should have received his fifty-year bar at the same time, but did not in fact receive it until 24 June 1944.

The unique award of a sixty-year bar to a George V Medal should also be mentioned here. This was on 2 April 1970 to Ephraim James Rainbow, Chief Cabinet Maker and latterly Curator of Pictures at Hampton Court.

Whereas the two fifty-year bars were struck from dies prepared at the Royal Mint, (and a good number of fifty-year bars have subsequently been awarded) the sixty-year bar, which will never be awarded again, was specially engraved.

GEORGE VI LONG AND FAITHFUL SERVICE MEDAL, (1st type) obverse as worn by a woman. Reverse, both types.

(*left*) E.J. RAINBOW MVO, Chief Cabinet Maker, later Curator of Pictures, at Hampton Court, the unique recipient of a sixty-year bar to his Long and Faithful Service Medal, which was awarded in 1930.

GEORGE VI LONG AND
FAITHFUL SERVICE
MEDALS, 2nd type
obverse *(above)* and
obverse engraved as for
broken service *(below)*.

ELIZABETH II LONG
AND FAITHFUL
SERVICE MEDALS: *(left)*
obverse 1st type; *(centre)*
reverse 1st and 2nd
type; *(right)* obverse 2nd
type, where there has
been broken service;
(bottom) obverse 2nd
type, as worn by a lady.

Final approval of the specimen George VI Long and Faithful Service Medal, was not obtained from the King until early December 1943. It was anticipated by the Privy Purse that about 50 medals would be required in the first instance. A list of 38 names was immediately sent to the Mint for medals to be named and engraved with appropriate dates and these medals were delivered to Buckingham Palace on 23 December. A further 73 medals were ordered from the Mint on that same day. These were all for outdoor staff employed on the King's private estates at Sandringham and Balmoral and at the Royal Gardens and Farms at Windsor. Though not mentioned in the Warrant, it was decided that broken service, as long as the full 20 years were served, could count for a medal. Medals awarded in these circumstances were engraved with just one date on the suspension bar.

Instead of creating a new medal ribbon it was decided to use the George V medal ribbon in reverse, so that the stripes should now run from top right to bottom left.

One award of King George VI's medal was made after the King's death in 1952. It was presented by the Queen to Mr James Macdonald who had been assistant Valet to the King prior to his accession and throughout the reign, so that it was thought appropriate that he should receive a George VI medal. It was perhaps not anticipated that Macdonald would then go on to be Valet to the Duke of Edinburgh and when he qualfed for the forty-year bar to his medal in 1972 he was by then Valet to the Prince of Wales.

In November 1952 initial moves were made for the institution of Queen Elizabeth II's Long and Faithful Service Medal. As they had in 1936, with the cypher of Edward VIII, the Royal Mint proposed a modification of the

Queen's cypher in the George V style to enable it to be fitted more comfortably around the rim of the medal (see illustration). In the event, this proposal was set aside in preference for a wholly new design. By placing it in a concave-sided box the new cypher could be used unchanged. This was submitted to the Queen and received her approval. The obverse of the medal bore the uncrowned laureated bust of Her Majesty which appeared on the coinage and was designed by Mrs Mary Gillick CBE. Apart from the modification of the legend the obverse has remained unchanged. The ageless and elegant reverse, designed for George V's medal by W.H.J. Blackmore and used on George VI's medal, was also to remain unchanged.

In comparison to the elaborate ribbon of the Victoria Faithful Service Medal and the innovative and typically thirties design of the jacquard-striped ribbon used for the George V and George VI medals, the design chosen for the Queen's medal, using the same colours red and blue was rather simpler.

THE MEDALS of Cyril Dickman.

Illustrated is the unique combination of medals awarded to Cyril Dickman, the former Palace Steward. At his retirement audience with the Queen on 30 January 1990 he received the fifty-year bar to his Long and Faithful Service Medal, having entered service as Nursery Footman to the Princesses Elizabeth and Margaret in December 1940. He received the RVM silver in 1969, the gold medal in 1985 and the MVO in 1988, yet another fine example of long and loyal service to the monarch.

THE COVER OF THE
BOOKLET of the Rules
and Regulations of
The Victoria Faithful
Service Medal.

THE RULES AND REGULATIONS OF THE VICTORIA FAITHFUL SERVICE MEDAL

═══

I.

THE QUEEN, being desirous of rewarding those servants who have long faithfully and personally served Her Majesty, is pleased hereby to institute a Decoration to be conferred on such of The Queen's servants as Her Majesty may think fit, in appreciation of their long and faithful services to The Queen.

II.

In special cases the Medal may be conferred for faithful services, irrespective of the length of service.

III.

The Decoration shall be called "THE VICTORIA FAITHFUL SERVICE MEDAL."

IV.

It shall consist of a Medal, surmounted by the Royal Cypher and Imperial Crown above, all in Silver, which Medal shall bear on one side the Effigy of The Queen, and on the other the name of the Recipient, encircled by the Union Wreath of Roses, Thistles, and Shamrocks; the words "Presented by QUEEN VICTORIA" being engraved on the edge.

V.

And also of a Gold Medal of a similar size and form, with the words "VICTORIA DEVOTED SERVICE MEDAL" engraved on the edge. This Gold Medal will only be conferred by The Queen for very exceptional services.

VI.

A Servant who has been in possession of the above-mentioned silver Medal for ten years, will have the figure 10 added to the bar from which the Medal is suspended, and subsequently the figures 20 and 30, according to his length of service while holding the Medal.

VII.

The Medal is to be worn at the button-hole, or on the left breast, attached to a ribbon of Stuart tartan.

VIII.

"THE VICTORIA FAITHFUL SERVICE MEDAL" being founded by Queen Victoria, will always bear The Queen's Effigy upon it.

IX.

On the death of any Servant who possesses the Medal, it will become the property of his family; but no person, excepting the Servant on whom it was conferred, is on any account to wear the Medal.

X.

The institution of this Decoration, and these Rules, shall be duly recorded by the Lord Chamberlain of Her Majesty's Household; and the names of all the Recipients of the Medal, together with a brief account of their services, shall be entered in a book which shall be kept in the Office of the Lord Chamberlain.

By Command,
J.C. COWELL,
Master of Her Majesty's Household.

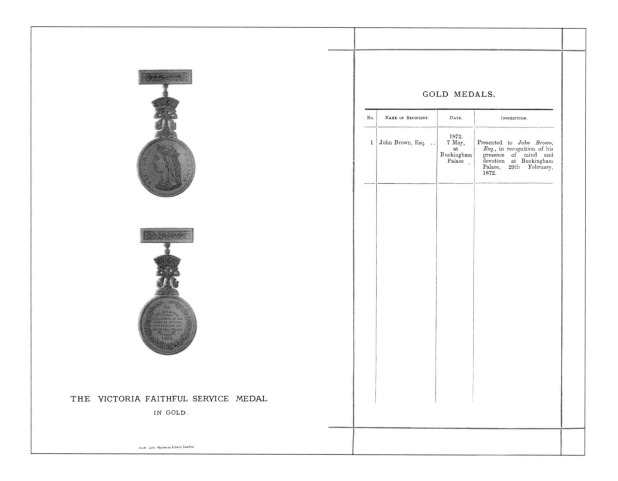

GOLD MEDALS.

No.	NAME OF RECIPIENT.	DATE.	INSCRIPTION.
1	John Brown, Esq. ..	1872. 7 May, at Buckingham Palace	Presented to *John Brown, Esq.*, in recognition of his presence of mind and devotion at Buckingham Palace, 29th February, 1872.

THE VICTORIA FAITHFUL SERVICE MEDAL
IN GOLD.

SILVER MEDALS.

No.	NAME OF RECIPIENT.	DATE.	INSCRIPTION.
1	*Rudolf Löhlein, Esq.* (*Died 19 Feb., 1896.*)	1872.	Presented by Queen Victoria to *Rudolf Löhlein, Esq.*, Her Majesty's Personal Attendant, for faithful services to the Prince Consort for 15 years, and to the Queen for 11 years. One bar for service.
2	*John Brown, Esq. ..* (*Died 27 March, 1883.*)	1872.	Presented by Queen Victoria to *John Brown, Esq.*, Her Majesty's Personal Attendant, for his constant, faithful, and devoted services to the Queen for 21 years. One bar for service.
3	*William Cullen, Esq.* (*Died 8 Nov., 1880.*)	1872.	Presented by Queen Victoria to *William Cullen, Esq.*, Clerk Comptroller of the Kitchen, for his faithful and zealous services during 42 years to the Queen and her Predecessor, King William IV.
4	*Mr. Spencer Cowley* (*Died 1 Jan., 1893.*)	1872.	Presented by Queen Victoria to *Mr. Spencer Cowley*, Jäger, for faithful services during 24 years to the Queen and the Prince Consort.
5	*George Fleming, Esq.* (*Died 3 March, 1895.*)	1872.	Presented by Queen Victoria to *George Fleming, Esq.*, Page of the Backstairs, for 42 years of faithful service to the Duchess of Kent and the Queen. One bar for service.

THE VICTORIA FAITHFUL SERVICE MEDAL
IN SILVER.

PAGES FROM THE BOOKLET of the Rules and Regulations of The Victoria Faithful Service Medal.

RECIPIENT OF THE DEVOTED SERVICE MEDAL

John Brown Esq.

1872, 7 May, at Buckingham Palace. Presented to John Brown, Esq., in recognition of his presence of mind and devotion at Buckingham Palace, 29th February 1872.

Born on 8 December 1826 at Crathienard, Aberdeenshire, second son of John Brown and Margaret Leys. Entered service as Gillie at Balmoral in August 1849; appointed to personal attendance on the Queen in Scotland 1858; Queen's Highland Attendant February 1865; Her Majesty's Personal Attendant 1873. Died at Windsor Castle 27 March 1883.

Brown must have been the recipient of several foreign awards during his service though no complete record has been discovered. However, it is known that he received two medals: the Hessian General Medal of Honour bearing on the obverse the head of Ludwig III and on the reverse the inscription 'For merit' 1 April 1880; this and his Gold and Silver (British) Medals are now contained in a specially made case by Wyon; the second foreign award was the Saxe-Coburg Medal of Merit of the Ducal Saxe-Ernestine House Order bearing the head of Ernest II (Gilt) 7 June 1882.

JOHN BROWN WITH HIS BROTHERS, Hugh (*left*) and William (*right*). Hugh was Highland Attendant to Queen Victoria 1891–8.

RECIPIENTS OF THE VICTORIA FAITHFUL SERVICE MEDAL

1 Rudolf Lohlein Esq.

1872. Presented by Queen Victoria to Rudolf Lohlein, Esq., Her Majesty's Personal Attendant, for faithful services to the Prince Consort for 15 years, and to the Queen for 11 years. One Bar for service.

Medal presented at Balmoral 24 May 1872. Rudolf John Bernhard Lohlein was born on 13 January 1827 at Niederfullbach, the son of William Lohlein, Forester at Fülbach, near Coburg. First employed as a Clerk in the Exchequer and Tax Office at Rodach, he later entered the Grand Ducal Saxe-Ernestine Household as a Footman. Entered Royal service in 1846 as 2nd Valet to Prince Albert from June 1847; in August 1858 Cart, the Prince Consort's principal valet, died and Lohlein took up the position until the Prince Consort died in December 1861;

RUDOLF LOHLEIN

was retained by Queen Victoria as her Personal Attendant and Groom of the Chambers until 1 July 1884 when he was pensioned, retaining the position of Extra Attendant. Lohlein, who became a naturalised British subject, married Elizabeth, daughter of Whitfield Collins at St George's, Hanover Square, on 11 July 1850. At first living in Pimlico, they were later given a house at Windsor Castle; they had 6 children, 3 boys and 3 girls. On his retirement, the Lohleins took a house in Surbiton, 'Santa Cruz' (which he later changed to 'Fülbach' after his birthplace), Surbiton Hill Park; later moved to 4 South Bank Terrace, Surbiton, where he died on 19 February 1896. His wife died 10 October the same year. Both were buried in St Mark's Churchyard, Surbiton.

2 John Brown Esq.

1872. Presented by Queen Victoria to John Brown, Esq., Her Majesty's Personal Attendant, for his constant, faithful, and devoted services to the Queen for 21 years.
One Bar for service.

Medal presented at Balmoral 24 May 1872. For details, see Devoted Service Medal above.

3 William Cullen Esq.

1872. Presented by Queen Victoria to William Cullen, Esq., Clerk Comptroller of the Kitchen, for his faithful and zealous services during 42 years to the Queen and her Predecessor, King William IV.

Medal presented at Windsor Castle 20 June 1872 (in first F.S.M. Booklet date given as 22 June). Born about 1813 in Chelmsford, Essex. Entered service of George IV 1830; listed in Imperial Calendar as Apprentice 1832, Under Clerk 1836, 4th Clerk of the Kitchen 1838, 3rd do., 1842, 2nd do. 1851, 1st do. 1855, Clerk Comptroller 1868; retired 1878. Died 8 November 1880 at the Royal Mews, Buckingham Palace, buried in Brompton Cemetery where there is a headstone. His son, William Cullen, MVO (January 1913) was Accountant in the Royal Mews, and died 30 March 1922. Refs.: *The Times* 17 November 1880. Cullen's Medal is in the Royal Collection at Windsor Castle.

WILLIAM CULLEN

4 Mr Spencer Cowley

1872. Presented by Queen Victoria to Mr Spencer Cowley, Jaeger, for faithful services during 24 years to the Queen and the Prince Consort

Medal presented at Balmoral 24 May 1872. Born about 1817 in Shropshire. At an early age became a mercenary in the Spanish Legion serving in Portugal and was present at the Battle of Oporto. Returning to Britain, he joined the Royal Horse Guards. Entered the service of the Prince Consort as Jaeger in January 1848; retired 1881. Died 1 January 1893, at the Cottage, Kensington Palace, buried in Ealing Cemetery (Grave No. 15 RD; there is no headstone). Also recipient of 1887 Jubilee Medal (Silver), and Portugal – Order of the Tower and Sword, and War Medal 1826–34 (Bronze).
Refs.: *The Times*, 4 January 1893; *Leaves from a Journal of Our Life in the Highlands.*

SPENCER COWLEY

5 George Fleming Esq.

1872. Presented by Queen Victoria to George Fleming, Esq., Page of the Backstairs for 42 years of faithful service to the Duchess of Kent and the Queen.
One Bar for service.

Medal presented at Windsor Castle 29 June 1872. Born 1 July 1816 at Buxted Park, Kent. Entered service of the Duchess of Kent 23 November 1830 and made Footman February 1835. Footman to Queen Victoria 21 June 1837; Assistant Gentleman Porter 20 January 1846; 3rd Page of the Presence 2nd Class December 1848, taking up his appointment on 15 January 1849; Page of the Backstairs 1 January 1854; Queen's Page 1868; retired 1886. Fleming married at St George's Hanover Square, 20 January 1839, Mary Ann Goldsmith, a servant at Buckingham Palace; they had 7 children. Formerly of Adelaide Cottage, Home Park, Windsor, he died 3 March 1895 at

GEORGE FLEMING

7 George Searle Esq.

1872. Presented by Queen Victoria to George Searle, Esq., Page of the Backstairs, for faithful services to the Queen during 30 years. Two Bars for service.

Medal presented at Balmoral 24 May 1872. George James Searle, born 1815. Footman to Princess Augusta 1836; Footman to the Queen 1842, Page of the Presence 1858, Page of the Backstairs 1859; retired June 1897 when he received the RVM (Silver) from the Queen; Recorded as receiving the Hessian Medal of Merit (Bronze) bearing the head of the Grand Duchess Alice on the occasion of the wedding of Princess Beatrice to Prince Henry of Battenburg 23 July 1885. Recipient of 1887 Jubilee Medal (Silver) and 1897 bar. Died 28 July 1901 at 17 Fitzwilliam Road, Clapham, Surrey. Buried in Norwood Cemetery (Grave No. 26388). Refs.: *The Times*, 29 July 1901. Son, Richard James Searle, also in Royal service; Clerk to the Master of the Household; died 1901.

GEORGE SEARLE

8 Stephen Maslin Esq.

1872. Presented by Queen Victoria to Stephen Maslin, Esq., Page of the Backstairs, for faithful services during 44 years to the Queen and her mother, the Duchess of Kent. One Bar for service.

Medal presented at Balmoral 24 May 1872. Born 4 June 1810 at Melksham, Wilts. Entered service of the Duchess of Kent and Princess Victoria 1 February 1828 as Steward's Room Man; Footman 1829, and Page 1838; on the death of the Duchess of Kent 16 March 1861, he

Victoria, 22 Woodhurst Road, Acton, and was buried in Brompton Cemetery (Grave AK 159153). Fleming is recorded as receiving the Hessian Medal of Merit (Bronze) bearing the head of the Grand Duchess Alice on the occasion of the wedding of Princess Beatrice to Prince Henry of Battenburg 23 July 1885. Refs.: *Windsor & Eton Express* 9 & 16 March 1895; *The Times*, 7 & 11 March 1895; *Daily Telegraph*, 8 & 11 March 1895; *The People*, 10 March 1895.

6 Gilbert Sprague Esq.

1872. Presented by Queen Victoria to Gilbert Sprague, Esq., Page of the Backstairs for faithful service to the Queen during 32 years.

Medal presented at Windsor Castle 20 June 1872 (in first F.S.M. Booklet date given as 28 June at Claremont). Born about 1811. Footman to the King of the Belgians from 1830 to 1840, then to the Prince Consort; listed in Imperial Calendar as Queen's Page 1859. Formerly of 19 High Street, Parish of Hanover Square; died 28 December 1873 at Brabant Villa, Thames Ditton, Surrey.

GILBERT SPRAGUE

STEPHEN MASLIN

entered the Queen's service as a super-numerary Page of the Backstairs on 1 April of that year; retired 31 December 1887. Died 14 November 1891 at 5 Glebe Place, Chelsea; Mrs Maslin was House-maid to the Duchess of Kent 1826–41 and died 19 April 1878 aged 70. Both buried in Windsor Cemetery. Maslin is recorded as receiving the Hessian Medal of Merit (Bronze) bearing the head of the Grand Duchess Alice on the occasion of the marriage of Princess Beatrice to Prince Henry of Battenburg, 23 July 1885. Refs.: *The Times*, 17 & 21 November 1891; *Windsor & Eton Gazette*.

9 Thomas Newell Esq.

1872. Presented by Queen Victoria to Thomas Newell, Esq., Page of the Backstairs for faithful services during 24 years to the Queen and the Prince Consort. One Bar for service.

Medal presented at Windsor Castle 20 June 1872. Born about 1822 at Little Bowden, Northants. Footman 1848; Sergeant Footman to the Prince Consort 1860, and to the Queen 1864; Page of the Backstairs 1867; pensioned 31 July 1888. Died 28 February 1899 at St James's Palace and buried in Brompton Cemetery (where there is a headstone); his wife,

THOMAS NEWELL

Harriet, died 13 May 1914 aged 92. He is recorded as receiving the Hessian Medal of Merit (Bronze) bearing the head of the Grand Duchess Alice on the occasion of the wedding of Princess Beatrice to Prince Henry of Battenburg 23 July 1885. Refs: *The Times*, 6 March 1899.

10 Richard Keys Taylor Esq.

1872 Presented by Queen Victoria to Richard Keys Taylor, Esq., Page of the Presence, for 32 years of faithful service to the Queen. One Bar for service.

RICHARD TAYLOR

Medal presented at Windsor Castle 20 June 1872. Born about 1818. Entered the Queen's service as Gentleman Porter 1839; 1st Groom Porter 1845, Page of the Presence 2nd Class 1846, 1st Class 1852; last listed 1891. Died 8 April 1899 at 45 Cambridge Street, Pimlico and buried Brompton Cemetery. Recorded as receiving the Hessian Medal of Merit (Bronze) bearing the head of the Grand Duchess Alice on the occasion of Queen Victoria's Jubilee, July 1887.

11 Edmund Heale Esq.

1872. Presented by Queen Victoria to Edmund Heale, Esq., First Clerk of the Kitchen, for 35 years of faithful service to the Queen. One Bar for service.

Medal presented at Balmoral 24 May 1872. Born about 1820. Entered Royal

EDMUND HEALE

service as Apprentice in the Kitchens 1837; First listed in Imperial Calendar, Fourth Clerk of the Kitchen 1843, Third Clerk 1851, 2nd Clerk 1855, 1st Clerk 1868, and Clerk Comptroller 1879. Died in service 11 September 1889 at Acacia, Albert Road, Battersea; buried in Brompton Cemetery where there is a headstone. Recorded as receiving the Hessian Medal of Merit (Bronze) bearing the head of the Grand Duchess Alice on the occasion of the wedding of Princess Beatrice to Prince Henry of Battenburg 23 July 1885. Refs.: *The Times*, 13 & 17 September 1889.

12 Mr Alphonse Gouffé

1872. Presented by Queen Victoria to Mr Alphonse Gouffé, Pastry Cook, for 32 years of faithful service to the Queen.

Medal presented at Windsor Castle 20 June 1872 (in first F.S.M. Booklet date given as 29 June at Claremont). Born about 1814 in Paris. Entered Royal service 1840 as Pastry Cook; retired 1881. Medal now in Robert B. Honeyman Jnr collection at Los Angeles County Museum of Natural History.

CHARLES GREEN

13 Mr Thomas Cocking

1872. Presented by Queen Victoria to Mr Thomas Cocking, Lamplighter, for faithful service to the Queen and her Predecessor, King William IV, for 43 years.

Medal presented at Windsor Castle 20 June 1872. Born about 1805. Entered Royal service 1829; 2nd Lamplighter 1845; 1st do.1865; Last listed in Imperial

Calendar. in 1879. Died 6 June 1900 at 28 Love Lane, Windsor. Refs.: *Windsor Chronicle*, 15 June 1900.

14 Mr Charles Green

1872. Presented by Queen Victoria to Mr Charles Green, Second Clerk of the Kitchen, for 33 years of faithful service to the Queen.   One Bar for service.

Medal presented at Windsor Castle 20 June 1872. Charles James Green, born 1823 at Elsenden, Herts. Entered Royal service as an Extra Assistant in the Cellars October 1838; 2nd Yeoman 1851, 1st Yeoman 1858, 2nd Clerk of the Kitchen 1867, 1st Clerk 1880; retired 1882. Died 11 November 1887 at 48 Belleville Road, Battersea.

15 Mr John Grant

1873. Presented by Queen Victoria to Mr John Grant, Head Keeper at Balmoral, for faithful service to the Queen and the Prince Consort during 26 years.

Medal presented at Balmoral 24 May 1873. Born 17 November 1810 in Auchindryne, Braemar . Entered service as Gillie to Sir Robert Gordon 1832 and in 1839 was made a Keeper, holding the situation until the death of Sir Robert in 1847, when he entered Royal service with the Queen and Prince Consort; pensioned

JOHN GRANT

in 1875. Married in 1841 Elizabeth Robbie and had 6 sons and 1 daughter. Died 17 November 1878 and buried at Braemar. three children were in Royal service: Arthur Patrick Grant succeeded Donald Stewart as Head Keeper at Balmoral 1901; retired 1924; died 28 July 1937. Alexander (see No. 83 below). Victoria, housekeeper at Balmoral. Refs.: *Leaves from a Journal of Our Life in the Highlands* and *More Leaves from a Journal of a Life in the Highlands*.

16 Mr John Kraeusslach

1873. Presented by Queen Victoria to Mr John Kraeusslach, Head Groom, for faithful services to the Queen and the Prince Consort during 32 years.

Medal presented at Windsor Castle 22 June 1873. John Nicholas Kraeusslach, born 1820 in Salzburg, Germany. Entered the service of the Prince Consort as Groom 1840; formerly in the service of the Prince's father. Died in service at the Royal Mews, Windsor Castle, 7 February 1876, buried Brompton Cemetery (Grave No. 17869 AC 200 x 18). A son, E. Kraeusslach, entered the Royal Mews in 1876 and became one of the Queen's Postillions; he died of rheumatic fever 31 December 1897 while still in service. Refs.: *The Times*, 13 February 1876; *Windsor & Eton Express*, 12 February 1876.

ALPHONSE GOUFFÉ   JOHN KRAEUSSLACH

17 Mr Charles Smith

1873. Presented by Queen Victoria to Mr Charles Smith, State Coachman, for faithful services to the Queen during 29 years.

Medal presented at Windsor Castle 7 July 1873. Born about 1810 in Kersey, Norfolk. Entered Royal service in 1844, Died 20 January 1898.

18 Mr John Wagland

1873. Presented by Queen Victoria to Mr John Wagland, Coachman, for faithful services during 42 years to the Queen and her Predecessor, King William IV.

Medal presented at Windsor Castle 20 June 1873. John George Wagland. Born 1814 at Charing Cross. Entered service of William IV as Postillion 2 February 1831; Assistant Coachman 1847, Coachman 1854; retired 1879. Died 24 July 1892 at Queen's Cottage, Bushey Park, Teddington, Middx. His father, grandfather and daughter were all in Royal service; his grandfather entered service of George III in 1788 and his father, also John Wagland, in January 1807 as a Helper in the Royal Mews; promoted Postillion 1812, serving both George IV and William IV; promoted Assistant Coachman 1831, and Porter 1840 at the Royal Mews, Windsor. His daughter, Emily Wagland, was for a time employed as Nursery Maid to the Prince of Wales's children. Refs.: *Surrey Comet*, 30 July 1892; *Leaves from a Journal of Our Life in the Highlands.*

JOHN CANNON

19 Mr John Cannon

1873. Presented by Queen Victoria to Mr John Cannon, Coachman, for faithful services during 40 years to the Queen and her predecessor, King William IV.

Medal presented at Windsor Castle 20 June 1873. Born about 1821 at Eton. Entered service of William IV 1833. Died 12 October 1883 at Sunningdale. Refs.: *Windsor & Eton Express*, 27 October 1883.

GEORGE BOURNER

20 Mr George Bourner

1873. Presented by Queen Victoria to Mr George Bourner, the Queen's Postillion, for faithful services to the Queen during 28 years. One Bar for service.

Medal presented at Balmoral 24 May 1873. Born about 1821 in Wimbledon. Entered service of the Queen as Helper March 1845; Postillion 1862, the Queen's Postillion 1865, later Head Coachman. Died 1 May 1895 at Surrey Cottage, East Cowes, Isle of Wight, and buried in East Cowes Cemetery. His son, Samuel Bourner, was also Queen's Postillion; died 28 November 1896 aged 43, and buried in Windsor Cemetery. Refs.: *Isle of Wight and Cowes Visitors Directory*, 3 & 10 May 1895; *Victoria Travels* by David Duff, p.226.

21 Samuel Shepperd, Esq.

1873. Presented by Queen Victoria to Samuel Shepperd, Esq., State Page, for faithful services during 43 years to the Queen and her Predecessor, King William IV.

Medal presented at Windsor Castle 20 June 1873. Born about 1794. Entered the service of King William IV 1830 as a Page of the Presence 2nd Class; Page of the Backstairs 1841, State Page 1844. Died 6 August 1874 at 77 Gloucester Street, Pimlico.

JOHN WAGLAND

SAMUEL SHEPPERD

JOSEPH HILL

22 Joseph Hill, Esq.

1873. Presented by Queen Victoria to Joseph Hill, Esq., State Page for faithful service during 39 years to the Queen and her Predecessor, King William IV.
One Bar for service.

Medal presented at Windsor Castle 20 June 1873. Born 1810; entered service of King William IV 1834 as Footman; Footman to Queen Victoria 1837; Page of the Presence 2nd Class 1852; State Page 1862. Died on 21 December 1884 at 3 Sussex Street, Pimlico.

23 William Tuppen Esq.

Presented by Queen Victoria to William Tuppen, Esq., Page of the Presence, for faithful services during 44 years to the Queen and her mother, the Duchess of Kent.
One Bar for service.

WILLIAM TUPPEN

Born 1813. Entered the service of the Duchess of Kent 1829; on her death in 1861, transferred to the Queen's service as a supernumerary Page of the Presence 2nd Class; Page of the Presence 2nd Class 1863; 1st Class 1867, and State Page 1877; retired 1888. Died on 24 December 1890 at 31 Griffin Road, Plumstead, Kent.

24 Mr William Peel

1873. Presented by Queen Victoria to Mr William Peel, Messenger in attendance on the Queen, for faithful services to the Queen during 31 years. One Bar for service.

Medal presented at Balmoral on 24 May 1873. Born 1812. Entered service of Queen Victoria 1841; Page of the Presence 1841; Messenger in attendance on the Queen 1851; retired 1884. Died 28 April 1887 at 73 Eaton Terrace, Eaton Square, London.

25 Mr Charles Frederick Jungbluth

1873. Presented by Queen Victoria to Mr Charles Jungbluth, First Master Cook, for faithful services to the Queen during 26 years. One Bar for service.

CHARLES JUNGBLUTH

Medal presented at Balmoral 24 May 1873. Born 1821 as Frederick August Carl Philipp Jungbluth. Entered service of Queen Victoria 1847; first listed as German Cook 1848; 3rd Master Cook 1854; 2nd Master Cook 1866; 1st Master Cook 1869; pensioned 1887. Died

WILLIAM PEEL

12 August 1895 at 83 Broomwood Road, Wandsworth Common, London. His son Walter Julius William George Jungbluth, a Clerk in Holy Orders, lived at Leesfield Vicarage, Oldham. Refs.: *More Leaves from a Journal of a Life in the Highlands.*

26 Mr John Mountford

1873. Presented by Queen Victoria to Mr John Mountford, Second Master Cook, for faithful services during 44 years to the Queen and her mother, the Duchess of Kent.

JOHN MOUNTFORD

Medal presented at Windsor Castle 20 June 1873. Born at Kensington about 1821. Entered service c.1829; first listed as Larderer and Storer 1844; Yeoman of the Kitchen 1845; 4th Master Cook 1854; 3rd Master Cook 1866; 2nd Master Cook 1870; pensioned 1880. Appointed a Groom of the Great Chamber until his death on 19 May 1896 at 11 Ditchling Rise, Preston, nr. Brighton; buried in Brighton and Preston Cemetery.

27 Mr Thomas Naldrett

1873. Presented by Queen Victoria to Mr Thomas Naldrett, Head Groom, for faithful services to the Queen during 27 years. Two Bars for service.

Medal presented at Windsor Castle 20 June 1873. Born 1833 the 7th son of George Naldreth of 'Cradles', Warnham, Sussex. Entered service of Queen Victoria in 1846; retired 1896. Died 3 May 1906 at 43 King's Road, Windsor; buried in St Mary's Churchyard, Slough. Refs.: *Windsor & Eton Express*, 5 & 12 May 1906.

THOMAS NALDRETT

28 Henry Gibbs Esq.

1874. Presented by Queen Victoria to Henry Gibbs, Esq., Queen's Messenger, for faithful services to the Queen during 32 years. One Bar for service.

Medal presented at Balmoral 24 May 1874. Born 1814. Entered service of Queen Victoria as Footman 1842; Sergeant Footman 1854; Gentleman Porter

1860; Page of the Presence 1861; Queen's Messenger 1864. Died 28 October 1888 at 81 Salcott Road, Wandsworth, London.

29 Mr George Frederick De Saulles

1874. Presented by Queen Victoria to Mr George Frederick De Saulles, Fourth Master Cook, for faithful services to the Queen during 36 years.

GEORGE DE SAULLES

HENRY GIBBS

JOHN ROBERT HUDSON

Medal presented at Windsor Castle 26 June 1874. Born in Pimlico, London, about 1823. Entered service of Queen Victoria 1838; first listed as Apprentice in the Kitchen 1839; promoted to Larderer and Storer 1845; Yeoman of the Kitchen 1854; 4th Master Cook 1870; 3rd Master Cook 1877; 2nd Master Cook 1881. Died 7 November 1881 at 88 Dalyell Road, Brixton. Medal now in the American Numismatic Society Collection, New York.

30 Mr John Robert Hudson

1874. Presented by Queen Victoria to Mr John R. Hudson, Groom Porter, for faithful services to the Queen and her Predecessor, King William IV during 39 years. One Bar for service.

Medal presented at Windsor Castle 26 June 1874. Born 1820. Entered service as Steward's Room man 1835; Lamplighter 1839; Footman 1848; Assistant Gentleman Porter 1867; Groom Porter 1868; Yeoman Gentleman Porter 1877; 1st Gentleman Porter 1887. Died 29 October 1888 at 19 Shaftesbury Road, Hammersmith.

31 Mr Donald Stewart

1874. Presented by Queen Victoria to Mr Donald Stewart, Keeper at Balmoral, for faithful services to the Queen during 26 years. Two Bars for service.

DONALD STEWART

Medal presented at Balmoral 24 May 1874. Born 1826 at Bualtich, a farm on the Abergeldie Estate, the son of Donald Stewart and Mary Gordon. In 1846 entered the service of Sir Robert Gordon as Stable Helper and Assistant Keeper. Entered the service of Queen Victoria on 8 September 1848 as Keeper, later Head Keeper. Married to Margaret Thomson in 1853, the sister of Nos. 77 & 93 below. Died 10 August 1909 aged 83. Buried at Crathie. In a photograph of 1901 he wears the following 7 medals: RVM in Silver (Victoria); 1887 Jubilee with Bar 1897 in silver; FSM; Greece – George 1st Royal Household Medal (?silver); Saxe-Coburg – Cross of Merit of the Ducal Saxe Ernestine House Order (?silver); Coburg – Alfred and Marie Silver Jubilee Medal 1899 (silver); Hesse – Alice Medal (gilt) of 25 June 1891.

32 Mr Peter Farquharson

1874. Presented by Queen Victoria to Mr Peter Farquharson, Keeper at Balmoral, for faithful services to the Queen during 25 years.

Medal presented at Balmoral 20 May 1874. Born 1804. Entered service 1849. Died 25 May 1874 and buried at Crathie.

33 Mr John Kirby

1874. Presented by Queen Victoria to Mr John Kirby, Principal Table Decker, for faithful services to the Queen during 30 years. Two Bars for service.

Medal presented at Windsor Castle 4 July 1874. Born 1823 at Ashby, Northamptonshire. Entered service 1844; first listed in Imperial Calendar as Waxfitter 1847, and in 1848 as Assistant Table Decker; in 1849 as Waxfitter again; promoted 3rd Table Decker 1852, 2nd Table Decker 1860, Principal Table Decker 1872; Retired 1900. Died 7 November 1900 at 5 Elm Grove, Worple Road, Wimbledon. Buried in Wimbledon Cemetery (now known as 'Gap Road' Cemetery), Grave No AA/A/57, where there is a headstone. Kirby also had the following medals, Queen Victoria's Jubilee Medal 1887 (Silver) with bar 1897, Saxe-Coburg Duke Alfred Merit Medal, (Gilt) Siam, Royal Service Medal, King Chulalongkorn (Silver). Refs.: *The Times*, 12 November 1900, and *Surrey Independent and Mid-Surrey Standard*, 17 November 1900.

34 Joseph Julius Kanné, Esq.

1874. Presented by Queen Victoria to Joseph Julius Kanné, Esq., Director of Continental Journeys, for faithful services to the Queen during 14 years. One Bar for service.

Medal presented at Osborne 7 August 1874. Born in Pilsen 1818. Employed by the Queen and Prince of Wales as a courier on an *ad hoc* basis from 1850, and taken into the full time service of the Queen November 1860. Kanné is reported to have had 21 foreign orders; the following is a list of those awards he is known definitely to have been awarded: Queen Victoria's Jubilee Medal 1887, Denmark Knight of the Order of Dannebrog 9 November 1867, Sweden Knight of the Order of Vasa 1868, Hesse Knight 2nd Class of the Order of Philip 18 February 1878. Died 24 April 1888 at 45 Dover Street, W1; buried in Brompton Cemetery, where the headstone was erected by the Queen; the Queen was represented at the funeral by Sir Henry Ponsonby and Major Bigge, and the Prince of Wales attended himself. Refs.: *The Times*, 1 May 1888; *Windsor & Eton Express*, 5 May 1888; *The Jewish*

JOSEPH KANNÉ

Chronicle, 3 October 1947. *Illustrated London News*, 23 June 1888; *Daily Telegraph*, 1 May 1888.

35 Christian Doll, Esq.

1875. Presented by Queen Victoria to Christian Doll, Esq., Page of the Presence, for faithful services during 41 years to the Queen and her Predecessor, King William IV.

CHRISTIAN DOLL

Christian Philip Doll. Medal presented at Windsor Castle 22 June 1875. Born 1811 at Kirn a/d Nahe Rhein, Prussia. Entered service of William IV 1834; Baker to HM 1834; Page of the Presence 1852; Page of the Presence 1st Class 1866; last listed in Imperial Calendar 1882. Died at 79 Sloane Street, Middlesex, 21 December 1903 aged 92.

36 Mr John Carver

1875. Presented by Queen Victoria to Mr John Carver, Queen's Messenger, for faithful services during 31 years to the Queen and the Prince Consort. One Bar for service.

Medal presented at Balmoral 24 May 1875. Born 1825. Footman 1844; Sergeant Footman to the Prince Consort 1857, to HM 1860; Page of the Presence 1864; Messenger in attendance on HM 1870; last listed in Imperial Calendar 1889. Died at 105 Salcott Road, Battersea, 9 January 1889 aged 64.

JOHN CARVER

37 Mr Gottlob Waetzig

1875. Presented by Queen Victoria to Mr Gottlob Waetzig. Third Master Cook, for faithful services to the Queen during 37 years.

Medal presented at Windsor Castle 3 July 1875. Gottlob Alfred Waetzig, born about

GOTTLOB WAETZIG

1823, son of Johann Gottlob Waetzig, a musician of Swedish descent who had come to England from Dresden in 1815 and joined the Prince Regent's Band at Brighton, continuing in the bands of George IV and William IV. He subsequently became Bandmaster of the Second Lite Guards for eleven years retiring in 1849. Waetzig is first listed in the Imperial Calendar as an Apprentice in the Kitchen 1839, 2nd Yeoman of the Kitchen 1845, 1st Yeoman 1854, 4th Master Cook 1866, 3rd Master Cook 1870. Retired on pension 1876. Died at 344 Merton Road, Wandsworth, 5 December 1906. Mrs Waetzig (formerly Miss Greatress) was Dresser to the Queen until 1842. Two brothers Johann Gustav and Charles Adolphus were members of Queen Victoria's Band, the latter was to become Bandmaster of the 3rd Prince of Wales's Dragoon Guards; Augusta, his only sister ran a school at Brentford.

38 Mr James Attew

Presented by Queen Victoria to Mr James Attew, Queen's Messenger, for faithful services during 35 years to the Queen and the Prince Consort.

Medal presented at Balmoral 18 June 1875. Born 1817. Entered service 1840; retired 1884. Died at 46 Jervis Road, Fulham, 26 June 1889, and buried in Brompton Cemetery. Refs.: *St. James's Gazette*, 18 May 1889.

39 Mr George Pearson

1875. Presented by Queen Victoria to Mr George Pearson, Postillion, for faithful services to the Queen during 35 years.
One Bar for service.

Medal presented at Windsor Castle 22 June 1875. Born in Middlesex 1827. Entered service of the Queen 1840; Postillion at time of award, and employed as a Lamplighter at Windsor when awarded Bar in 1885. Died at 15 Railway Terrace, Slough, on 30 September 1897, and buried in Windsor Cemetery. Refs.: *Windsor & Eton Express*, 9 October 1897.

40 Mr William Goring

1875. Presented by Queen Victoria to Mr William Goring, Yeoman of the Silver Pantry, for faithful services to the Queen during 36 years.

Medal presented at Windsor Castle 22 June 1875. Born 1818; entered service of Queen Victoria 1839; first listed as Assistant in Silver Pantry 1845; Groom of the Silver Pantry 1854, and Yeoman 1860. Died at 22 Trinity Place, Windsor, 9 March 1881, and buried in Clewer Churchyard. Refs.: *Windsor & Eton Express*, 12 and 19 March 1881.

JAMES ATTEW

WILLIAM GORING

41 Mr Edward Collins

1875. Presented by Queen Victoria to Mr Edward Collins, Sergeant Footman, for faithful services to the Queen during 22 years. Two Bars for service.

Medal presented at Balmoral 24 May 1875. Edward Richard Collins, born at Hurstmonceux, Sussex, 1826; entered service 1853 as Footman; Sergeant Footman to the Queen 1864; Messenger to the Queen 1878; retired 1898 in consequence of his failing eyesight; the Queen had sent him to Germany for treatment but the operation he underwent did

EDWARD COLLINS

not have any lasting effect. Later lived at Hurstmonceux, New Road, Windsor, and died on 16 May 1902 at Holloway Sanatorium, Virginia Water; buried at Clewer Churchyard near Windsor. Recorded as receiving the Hessian Medal for Merit (Bronze), bearing head of the Grand Duchess Alice on the occasion of Queen Victoria's Jubilee 1887. Refs.: *Windsor & Eton Express*, 24 May 1902.

42 Mr John Cocking

1875. Presented by Queen Victoria to Mr John Cocking, Lamplighter, for faithful services to the Queen during 37 years.

Medal presented at Windsor Castle 22 June 1875. Born in London 1804. Entered service of Queen Victoria 1838 as Assistant Lamplighter, a post he held until pensioned in 1876. Died 29 April 1889 at 128 Radcliffe Road, Southampton.

43 Mr Thomas Hollis

1876. Presented by Queen Victoria to Mr Thomas Hollis, First Yeoman of the Kitchen, for faithful services to the Queen during 28 years. One Bar for service.

Medal presented at Balmoral 24 May 1876. Born 1828. Entered service of Queen Victoria as an Apprentice in the Kitchen; entered service with the

THOMAS HOLLIS

Duchess of Kent 1851, and on her death in 1861 re-entered the Queen's service; listed as Assistant Cook 1854, 2nd Yeoman of the Kitchen 1866, 1st Yeoman 1870, 4th Master Cook 1877, 3rd Master Cook 1881, 2nd Master Cook 1882, 1st Master Cook 1888, and Chief Cook 1889; retired 1891. Died 21 February 1905 at Leahurst, Normanton, Derbyshire. Recorded as receiving the Hessian Medal of Merit (Bronze), bearing the head of the Grand Duchess Alice 26 January 1888.

EUGÈNE THIOU

44 Eugène Thiou Esq.

1876. Presented by Queen Victoria to Eugène Thiou, Esq., Chief Cook, for faithful services to the Queen during 22 years. One Bar for service.

Medal presented at Windsor Castle 23 June 1876. Entered service of Queen Victoria in 1854; first listed as 2nd Master Cook 1855, 1st Master Cook 1866, Chief Cook 1870, and last listed 1888.

45 Mr William Ross

1876. Presented by Queen Victoria to Mr William Ross, Piper, for faithful services to the Queen during 22 years. One Bar for service.

Medal presented at Balmoral 24 May 1876. Born 27 March 1823 at Knockbairn, Ross-shire. Enlisted in 42nd Highlanders (Black Watch) March 1839, and served in

WILLIAM ROSS

Corfu, Malta and Bermuda; was appointed Pipe Major and Piper to the Queen 10 May 1854. He was responsible for a standard work on pipe music which ran to two editions, containing music much of which had never appeared in print before. Died in service on 10 June 1891 aged 68 at Crathie Villas, Clewer, near Windsor, and buried in Windsor Cemetery where there is a headstone. Recorded as having received the Hessian Medal of Merit (Bronze), bearing the head of the Grand Duchess Alice, on the occasion of the Queen's visit to Darmstadt 25 April 1890. Refs.: *Daily Telegraph*, 13 June 1891; *The Times*, 12 & 16 June 1891; *Windsor and Eton Express*, 20 June 1891. Ross's medal sold by Sotheby's 9 July 1975; other piping medals sold by Glendining's 13 February 1980.

46 Mr Edward Doe

1876. Presented by Queen Victoria to Mr Edward Doe, Postillion, for faithful services to the Queen during 26 years.
One Bar for service.

Medal presented at Windsor Castle 23 June 1876. Born in Windsor 1836. Entered service of Queen Victoria 1850 in the Royal Mews later becoming a Postillion. Died 4 January 1911 at Slough, Bucks.

FREDERIC WAGENRIEDER

47 Frederic Wagenrieder Esq.

1876. Presented by Queen Victoria to Frederic Wagenrieder, Esq., Page of the Chamber, for faithful services to the Queen during 22 years. Two Bars for service.

Charles Frederick Wagenrieder. Born 1820. Entered service of Queen Victoria 1854; appointed Page of the Chambers 31 January 1855 until May 1884 when he became Extra Page of the Chambers; State Page 1886 and continued as such until 1904. Died 4 December 1906 at 41 Harvard Road, Gunnersbury, Middx., and buried in Chiswick Old Church Cemetery. Refs.: *The Times*, 8 December 1906.

EDWARD DOE

48 Mr William Hislop

1877. Presented by Queen Victoria to Mr William Hislop, Groom Porter, for faithful services to the Queen during 28 years.
One Bar for service.

Born 1832. Entered service of Queen Victoria in the Master of the Horse's Department 1 July 1849; appointed Livery Assistant in the Silver Pantry, Lord Steward's Department 1 October 1853; moved back to the Master of the Horse's Department 30 April 1860 as Under Butler; Gentleman Porter 1 February 1876; Groom Porter 1877; Yeoman Gentleman Porter 1887 and 1st Gentleman Porter 1893. He lived at 36 Lindore Road, Battersea Rise, and died 13 May 1895 at St George's Hospital, Middx. Recorded as receiving the Hessian Medal of Merit (Bronze), bearing the head of the Grand Duchess Alice 25 June 1891.

GEORGE PAYNE

49 Mr George Payne

1877. Presented by Queen Victoria to Mr George Payne, State Coachman, for faithful services to the Queen during 39 years. One Bar for service.

Born in Pimlico 1823. Entered service of Queen Victoria 2 August 1838; appointed Established Helper 1 July 1852; Coachman 1 November 1858, and State Coachman 1 January 1876; retired in 1890.

50 Mr George Gower

1877. Presented by Queen Victoria to Mr George Gower, Groom, for faithful services to the Queen and her Predecessor, King William IV, during 42 years.
One Bar for service.

GEORGE GOWER

Born in Hampton 19 January 1821. Entered service of King William IV in 1835 as a Groom. Died at Derby Villa, Albany Road, Windsor, 25 February 1895, and buried in Windsor Cemetery where there is a headstone. Was a nephew of W. H. Gower (No. 76 below).

51 Mr James Long

1877. Presented by Queen Victoria to Mr James Long, Gate Porter, for faithful services to the Queen and her Predecessor, King William IV during 44 years.
One Bar for service.

Born in London 1821. Entered service of King William IV 1833 and was retained by Queen Victoria in 1837 as an Outrider; later Gateporter at the Lodge Gate in St.

JAMES LONG

Alban's Street, Windsor until 1888 when, owing to a succession of family bereavements, his mind became unhinged and he had to be confined at Peckham House Lunatic Asylum; died there 16 January 1890; by command of the Queen his body was brought back to the Mews at Windsor prior to his funeral; buried in Windsor Cemetery where on the headstone is recorded the death of his wife Elizabeth (died 3 June 1888 aged 67), Edward Long his son (died 30 January 1888 aged 32) who was also in the Queen's service for 17 years, and Frederick George Sayer his son-in-law (died 28 April 1888 aged 47) also having served the Queen 35 years. A recipient of the 1887 Jubilee Medal in Bronze. Ref.: *Windsor & Eton Express*, 18 & 25 January 1890.

52 Mr John Mackenzie

1877. Presented by Queen Victoria to Mr John Mackenzie, Keeper at Balmoral, for faithful services to the Queen and the Prince Consort during 27 years.
One Bar for service.

Born 1814. Entered service of Queen Victoria in 1850 as Keeper, later becoming Gatekeeper at the Bridge of Dee. Died at the Bridge of Dee Cottage, Braemar, 24 January 1895, and buried in Crathie Cemetery.

53 William Seabrook Esq.

1879. Presented by Queen Victoria to William Seabrook, Esq., Inspector at Windsor Castle, for faithful services to the Queen and her Predecessors, King George IV and King William IV and to the Duchess of Kent, during 45 years.

WILLIAM SEABROOK

Born 1813. Entered service of George IV in 1824; received his Warrant of appointment 1 January 1828; transferred by William IV to Master of the Horse's Department 1832, and to the Household of the Duchess of Kent 1840; appointed Inspector of Windsor Castle in September 1861; retired 1883. Died 3 October 1893 and buried in Windsor Cemetery. Refs: *Windsor & Eton Gazette*, 14 October 1893.

EDWARD COLLINS

54 Edward P. Collins Esq.

1879. Presented by Queen Victoria to Edward P. Collins, Esq., Inspector at Buckingham Palace, for faithful services to the Queen and her Predecessor, King William IV, during 47 years.
One Bar for service.

Edward Philip Gillam Collins, born 2 June 1816. Entered service of William IV; Tapissier at Buckingham Palace 1844; Windsor Castle 1854, and Osborne 1861; Inspector of Buckingham Palace 1876, when he was granted an apartment at Kensington Palace. Retired 1893. Died at Victor House, Partlands Avenue, Ryde, Isle of Wight 22 June 1903; buried in Whippingham Churchyard, near Osborne. Recorded as receiving the Hessian Medal of Merit (bronze), bearing the head of the Grand Duchess Alice 25 June 1891.

55 Mr William Miles

1879. Presented by Queen Victoria to Mr William Miles, Tapissier at Osborne, for faithful services to the Queen during 31 years.

WILLIAM MILES

HENRY TAIT

WILLIAM POWER

Born 1 March 1815. Employed on the Inspector's Staff at Windsor from 1848; appointed Tapissier at Windsor Castle 1862 and at Osborne 1876; retired December 1881 due to ill-health; drowned in the Thames at Clewer near Windsor 8 March 1882. His son George Edward Miles was in the Royal service, born 1852 and entered Lord Chamberlain's Department as Account Clerk 1875; Tapissier 1893, Inspector of Windsor Castle 1901–24; MVO (V) 30 October 1904, MVO (IV) 3 June 1924; also had Jubilee Medal 1887 (Silver) with bar 1897, Coronation Medals for 1902 (Silver) and 1911; Order of Villa Vicosa 4th Class (Portugal), Order of Naval Merit 5th Class (Spain), Order of the Vasa 5th Class (Sweden), Order of the Rising Sun 6th Class (Japan), Medal of the Order of the Crown of Prussia (Gilt); died 25 March 1942 (see *Who was Who*). Refs.: *Windsor & Eton Express*, 25 March, 1 & 22 April 1882.

56 Mr Henry Tait

1879. Presented by Queen Victoria to Mr Henry Tait, Bailiff of the Home and Shaw Farms, for faithful services to the Queen during 21 years.

Born near Kelso 13 October 1816. Entered service of Queen Victoria 1858 as Bailiff of the Home and Shaw Farms at

Windsor, having been in the service of the Duke of Sutherland at Dunrobin as Farm Superintendent for 20 years; in 1880 he was also put in charge of the Flemish Farm; died in service 22 April 1882 at Shaw Farm, Windsor, and buried in Windsor Cemetery. He was succeeded as Land Steward by his son William Henry Tait, MVO, born 16 April 1849, died 27 August 1909. Refs.: *Windsor & Eton Express*, 29 April 1882.

57 Mr James Brebner

1879. Presented by Queen Victoria to Mr James Brebner, Bailiff of the Norfolk and Flemish Farms, for faithful services to the Queen during 30 years.

Born 1805. Entered service of Queen Victoria in 1849 at Bagshot Park; appointed Bailiff of the Norfolk and Flemish Farms at Windsor in 1853; retired 1880. Died at Norfolk Farm, near Virginia Water, 14 January 1890; buried in Sunningdale Churchyard. Refs.: *Windsor & Eton Express*, 18 & 25 January 1890.

58 Mr William Power

1879. Presented by Queen Victoria to Mr William Power, Sergeant Footman, for faithful services to the Queen during 21 years. One Bar for service.

William Austin Power was born at Foots

Cray, Kent, 1837. Entered the service of Queen Victoria as Footman 1 January 1858; Sergeant Footman 26 April 1878, and one of the Queen's Own Messengers in May 1884. Died in service 28 October 1894 at Amerley House, Windsor, and buried in Windsor Cemetery where there is a headstone. Also had 1887 Jubilee Medal in Silver, Hesse – General Medal of Honour bearing head of Ludwig III Grand Duke of Hesse in Silver, 6 May 1884 on the occasion of the Queen's visit to Darmstadt for the marriage of Prince Louis of Battenburg to Princess Victoria of Hesse, Prussia – Medal of the Order of the Red Eagle (Silver). Refs.: *Windsor & Eton Gazette*, 2 November 1894; *Windsor & Eton Express*, 3 November 1894

59 Mr Adolphus Frederick William Lloyd

1880. Presented by Queen Victoria to Mr Adolphus Frederick William Lloyd, Second Clerk of the Kitchen, for faithful services to the Queen during 25 years.

Two Bars for service.

Born in Windsor 1830. Entered service of Queen Victoria in 1855 as 4th Clerk of the Kitchen, 3rd Clerk 1868, 2nd Clerk 1880, 1st Clerk 1883, Clerk Comptroller of the Kitchen 1890; retired 1901. Died at Montpelier Villas, Brighton, 12 December

ADOLPHUS LLOYD

– Royal Order of the Crown 4th Class (Warrant dated 9 May 1901), Hesse – Medal of Merit (Bronze) bearing head of the Grand Duchess Alice (July 1887), Russia – Medal for Zeal from Nicholas II (Gold, worn from the St Stanislas ribbon) (Warrant dated 1 May 1898 for services 22 September 1896), Prussia – Medal of the Order of the Red Eagle (Silver), Rumania – Medal of Merit (Gilt) (Warrant dated 11 November 1892), Saxe-Coburg – Medal of Merit of the Saxe Ernestine House Order, bearing the head of Ernest II (Gilt) (Warrant dated 29 December 1893). Waite was one of a very few servants who was left money in Queen Victoria's will, he received £70. Refs.: *The Times*, 15 November 1902; *Windsor & Eton Express*, 22 November 1902.

CHARLES AMBROSE

1905, buried in Norwood Cemetery. He is recorded in the *Windsor & Eton Express* as a recipient of the RVM (Silver) from Edward VII on 9 February 1901, but his name does not appear in the Register. He is known to have received the Order of the Red Eagle, 4th Class, from the Kaiser in 1890, and the Order of the Crown, 4th Class, in 1900; also Hesse – Medal of Merit (Bronze) bearing the head of the Grand Duchess Alice on the occasion of the Queen's Visit to Darmstadt 25 April 1890.

60 George Waite, Esq.

1880. Presented by Queen Victoria to George Waite, Esq., Page of the Presence, for faithful services to the Queen during 26 years. Two Bars for service.

Born 1834. Entered the service of Queen Victoria as Footman 7 May 1854; appointed 3rd Page of the Presence 2nd Class 10 December 1865, Page of the Presence 1st Class 1883, and Page of the Backstairs 1 January 1888; pensioned 23 July 1901. Died 14 November 1902 at Church Cottage, Newport Pagnell. Recipient of RVM (Silver) 1901, Jubilee Medal 1887 (Silver) and bar 1897, Prussia

GEORGE WAITE

61 Mr Henry Clark

1880. Presented by Queen Victoria to Mr Henry Clark, Lamplighter, for faithful services to the Queen during 43 years.

Born about 1821. Entered service of Queen Victoria in 1837 as Assistant Lamplighter; promoted 2nd Lamplighter 1865, and 1st Lamplighter 1880; retired 1885. Died 26 March 1891 at 133 Tyneham Road, Shaftesbury Park, Surrey.

62 Mr Charles Ambrose

1880. Presented by Queen Victoria to Mr Charles Ambrose, Porter, for faithful services to the Queen during 24 years. Two Bars for service.

Born about 1831. Entered service of Queen Victoria in 1856. First listed in the Imperial Calendar in 1890 as a Groom Porter promoted Yeoman Porter 1895; pensioned in 1901. Died 20 April 1908 at Gloucester Place, New Windsor.

63 Mr James Hannis

1880. Presented by Queen Victoria to Mr James Hannis, Yeoman Porter, for faithful services to the Queen during 26 years. One Bar for service.

Born Oxfordshire about 1827. Entered service of Queen Victoria in 1854; first listed in Imperial Calendar as Yeoman State Porter in 1877; retired 1895. Died 12 December 1897 at 63 Landor Road, Stockwell, Surrey, and buried in Windsor Cemetery

64 Mr David Bennett

1882. Presented by Queen Victoria to Mr David Bennett, Marshalman, for faithful services to the Queen during 45 years.

Born about 1820. Entered the service of Queen Victoria in 1837 as Assistant in the Steward's Room; appointed a Marshalman 1865. Died 21 January 1888.

65 Mr John West

1882. Presented by Queen Victoria to Mr John West, Coachman, for faithful services to the Queen during 44 years.

Born at Charing Cross, London, about 1822. Entered service of Queen Victoria 1 October 1838. Died 20 May 1894.

66 Mr Thomas Sands

1882. Presented by Queen Victoria to Mr Thomas Sands, Coachman, for faithful services to the Queen during 39 years.
                    One Bar for service.

Thomas Southgate Sands was born in Hendon in about 1829. Entered service of Queen Victoria 1843; promoted to State Postillion, later became Acting Coachman 16 August 1843, later Coachman in personal attendance on the Queen; he accompanied the Prince of Wales when at Oxford and Cambridge; having completed 50 years in the Royal service, the Queen presented him with a tea service and on his retirement in 1896 a massive silver teapot. Died at his home 'Lynmouth', Curzon Street, Slough, on 14 March 1906; buried in Slough Parish Churchyard. He had four sons all in Royal service: Thomas Southgate Sands, Storekeeper at Windsor Castle. William Southgate Sands, MVO, born 26 November 1853, entered Lord Chamberlain's Office, 1873; Inspector at Holyrood 1893–1906 and at Buckingham Palace 1900–24; died 13 December 1924. Henry Richard Sands, Chief Coal Porter at Buckingham Palace and Arthur Herbert Sands, Postillion, Royal Mews, Windsor. Refs: *Windsor & Eton Express*, 17 & 24 March 1906.

THOMAS SANDS

HENRY JARRETT

67 Mr Henry Jarrett

1882. Presented by Queen Victoria to Mr Henry Jarrett, Yeoman of the Cellars, for faithful services to the Queen during 24 years.

Born about 1837. Entered service of Queen Victoria 1858; Listed in Imperial Calendar. Messenger to the Lord Steward 1860, Messenger to the Board of the Green Cloth 1864, 2nd Yeoman of the Wine and Beer Cellars 1868, 1st Yeoman 1875, retired 1883. Appointed Groom of the Great Chamber 1879. Died 1 January 1890 at 1 Holyrood Villas, New Road, Clewer, near Windsor.

68 Mr Jean Nestor Tirard

1882. Presented by Queen Victoria to Mr Jean Nestor Tirard, Hairdresser to Her Majesty, for faithful services to the Queen during 36 years.

Jean Nestor Marie Tirard was born about 1820 in Lassy, Calvados, France. Appointed Hairdresser to Queen Victoria 1 October 1846; pensioned 1 October 1867. Resident at 39 Curzon Street, Mayfair; died at 10 Albert Terrace Margate 26 May 1888. Although Tirard

is recorded as retiring in 1867, he received his Medal in 1882. His son Nestor Isidore Charles Tirard was an eminent physician who became Emeritus Professor of Medicine, Kings College Hospital, London, was knighted in 1916, died 10 November 1928.

69 Mr William Kiddle

1883. Presented by Queen Victoria to Mr William Kiddle, Yeoman Porter, for faithful service to the Queen during 39 years.

Born 1807. Entered service of Queen Victoria 11 March 1844 as Footman; later promoted to Under Butler, and in 1873 Yeoman State Porter. Died at 69 Cambridge Street, Pimlico, 9 August 1883. Kiddle did not receive his Medal from the Queen personally as he was too ill to do so; it was sent to him on 25 May 1883 when it was feared he was about to die.

70 Mr Henry Manwaring

1883. Presented by Queen Victoria to Mr Henry Manwaring, Coachman, for faithful services to the Queen during 43 years.

Born in Parish of St George's, Hanover Square, 1827. Entered service of Queen Victoria 19 March 1840. Appointed Coachman 1 July 1864. State Coachman 1890. Pensioned 16 June 1890.

JEAN TIRARD

71 Mr Charles Michie

1885. Presented by Queen Victoria to Mr Charles Michie, Groom Porter, for faithful services to the Queen during 33 years.
    One Bar for service.

Born Crathie, Aberdeenshire 1828. Entered service of Queen Victoria 1852; first listed as Night Porter 1854, Wax Fitter 1860, 3rd Table Dresser 1866, Assistant Porter 1877, Groom Porter 1878, Yeoman Gentleman Porter 1889, 1st Gentleman Porter 1895; pensioned 1901.

72 Charles Robertson Esq.

1885. Presented by Queen Victoria to Charles Robertson, Esq., Page of the Presence, for faithful services to the Queen during 25 years.   One Bar for service.

Born about 1827. Entered service of the Prince Consort as Jaeger in July 1859; Page of the Presence 1865, State Page 1889; retired 1907.

CHARLES ROBERTSON

73 William Henry Blake, Esq.

1885. Presented by Queen Victoria to William Henry Blake, Esq., Page of the Presence, for faithful services to the Queen during 25 years.

Born about 1830. Entered service of Queen Victoria 1860 as Footman; Page of the Presence 2nd Class 7 February 1876,

1st Class 1889. Died 22 April 1895 at Hawthorn Lodge, Bushey Park, Teddington, Middx.

ARCHIBALD BROWN

74 Archibald Brown, Esq.

1885. Presented by Queen Victoria to Archibald Brown, Esq., Page of the Presence, for faithful services to the Queen during 22 years.   One Bar for service.

Archibald Anderson Brown, born October 1842, the youngest brother of John Brown, the Queen's Personal Attendant. Entered service of Queen Victoria at Windsor on 23 November 1863 as Steward's Room Waiter; promoted Wardrobe Man and Footman to Prince Leopold 8 August 1865, and Valet

WILLIAM BLAKE

in April 1866; (he married in 1872 Emma Johns who had been for some years one of Princess Louise's Dressers); appointed a Page of the Presence 2nd Class 1883, and a Page of the Backstairs 1889; pensioned 1901. In February 1901 received the RVM (Silver) from Edward VII. Died 28 December 1912 at 1 Cambridge Villas, New Road, Clewer, near Windsor, buried in the Windsor Cemetery where there is a headstone. He was left a legacy in Queen Victoria's will of £100. Refs.: *Highlanders of Scotland* by Kenneth Macleay (1870); *Windsor & Eton Express*, 11 May 1901 & January 1913.

75 Mr John Martin

1886. Presented by Queen Victoria to Mr John Martin, Yeoman of the Ewry, for 55 years of faithful services to the Queen and her Predecessor, King William IV.
    One Bar for service.

Born about 1819 in Brighton. Entered the service of King William IV in 1831 being employed in the Green Office; appointed Coal Porter August 1837, Head Coal Porter August 1839, Yeoman of the Ewry 1 October 1865; retired 1898. Was Groom of the Great Chamber 18 June 1881 until 1903. Recipient of 1887 Jubilee Medal (Silver) and 1897 bar, and 1902 Coronation Medal (Bronze). Formerly of Stanley Street, Pimlico. Died at Cornwall House, Cornwall Street, St George's Square, Middx 28 June 1903.

76 Mr William Henry Gower

1886. Presented by Queen Victoria to Mr William Henry Gower, Yeoman of the Silver Pantry, for faithful services to the Queen during 46 years.

Born 1826 in Hampton. Entered the service of Queen Victoria as an Assistant in the Steward's Room December 1840; appointed Wardrobe Footman to the Prince of Wales November 1850; 3rd Table Decker 1859; Yeoman of the Silver Pantry October 1865; 1st Yeoman April 1881. Died 5 August 1893 at 16 Brunswick Terrace, Windsor, buried in Windsor Cemetery. He was uncle of George Gower (No. 50 above), and father of Leonard Walter Gower (RVM 1923), who was also the son-in-law of John Heir (No. 100 below). Refs.: *Daily Telegraph*, 9 August 1893; *Windsor & Eton Express*, 12 August 1893.

77 Charles Thomson, Esq.

1886. Presented by Queen Victoria to Charles Thomson, Esq., Page of the Presence, for faithful services to the Queen during 26 years. One Bar for service.

Born on 25 August 1840 at Crathie the son of Charles Thomson, Post Master at Crathie. Entered the service of Queen Victoria first as a Gillie on the Royal Estate at Balmoral; in 1860 became a Helper in the Royal Mews at Buckingham Palace; Usher in the Steward's Room 1862, Footman 1864 (his Warrant as

Footman is dated two years later 9 March 1866); Page of the Presence 2nd Class 1 December 1883, Page of the Backstairs 1 April 1886; subsequently 2nd Page of the Backstairs 1 August 1888; pensioned 1901 when he received the RVM (Silver) from Edward VII. Died 14 June 1910 at 13 St Mark's Road, Windsor, buried in Windsor Cemetery. A recipient of the Jubilee Medal 1887 (Silver) and bar 1897, Russia – Nicholas II Medal for Zeal (Gold worn from the St Stanislas ribbon) 22 September 1896, Belgium – Leopold II Royal Household Medal (for servants of foreign Courts in Gilt) 11 February 1901, Rumania – Faithful Service Medal (Gilt) 24 December 1890, Saxe-Coburg – Medal of Merit of the Saxe-Ernestine House Order, bearing the head of Ernest II (Gilt) 24 April 1894, Hesse – Ludwig IV Medal of Merit (Bronze, small size medal) 23 July 1885 on the occasion of the marriage of Princess Beatrice to Prince Henry of Battenberg, Siam –Chulalongkorn Rajaruchi Medal, 5th Reign (Gilt).

Charles Thomson was one of 11 children, 7 of whom were employed in Royal service: Andrew, another Page of the Backstairs to Queen Victoria (No. 93 below); William, State Page to Edward

VII and George V (see RVM George V Silver); Alexander, Superintendent of Works at Osborne (see RVM Edward VII Silver); Tom, in charge of the Queen's Stables at Balmoral; John, in charge of the roads at Balmoral, later Head Forester; and Mary, Housekeeper to the Duke of Fife at Mar Lodge, who was married to Donald MacDonald, Gamekeeper to the Duke of Fife. Another sister, Margaret, married Donald Stewart, Headkeeper at Balmoral (No. 31 above); and another brother, Albert, succeeded his father as Post Master at Crathie, 1887–1933 when he was succeeded by his wife, Barbara, until her death in 1956; their son, Albert, was also Post Master. Refs.: *More Leaves from the Journal of a Life in the Highlands*; *Windsor & Eton Express*, 18 June 1910.

78 Mr John Lockwood

1886. Presented by Queen Victoria to Mr John Lockwood, Sergeant Footman, for faithful services to the Queen during 21 years.

Born 1842. Entered service of Queen Victoria in 1865 as Footman; Sergeant Footman 1884. Died in service 30 June 1888 at his home 2 St Mark's Place, Clewer, near Windsor. Recorded as receiving the Hessian General Medal of Honour (Silver) 'For Merit' Ludwig III 6 May 1884 on the occasion of the Queen's visit to Darmstadt for the wedding of Prince Louis of Battenberg to Prince Victoria of Hesse. Refs.: *Windsor & Eton Express*, 7 July 1888.

79 Mr William Whaley

1886. Presented by Queen Victoria to Mr William Whaley, Queen's Postillion, for faithful services to the Queen during 33 years. One Bar for service.

Born 28 January 1840 in Shoreditch, son of William Whaley, a coachman and Sarah Whaley (formerly Button). Entered the service of Queen Victoria on 18 June 1853, aged 13 years, as a postillion in the Royal Mews at Windsor Castle. He was placed on the established staff as an Established Helper 1 April 1876 and promoted to Queen's Postillion 1 January 1885; 1st Class Queen's Postillion 15 November 1887. Was promoted

CHARLES THOMSON   JOHN LOCKWOOD

WILLIAM WHALEY

Coachman 1 October 1888. He also received the Jubilee Medal 1887 in silver with '1897' bar and the Medal for Zeal of Montenegro in Silver; Pensioned in 1901, he died at 115 Salcott Road, South West Battersea on 17 September 1926.

80 Edward Lawley Esq.

1889. Presented by Queen Victoria to Edward Lawley, Esq., First Clerk of the Kitchen, for faithful services to the Queen during 25 years. One Bar for service.

Entered service of Queen Victoria on 7 April 1864 as an Apprentice in the Kitchen; appointed 4th Clerk of the Kitchen 1863, 3rd Clerk 1880, 2nd Clerk 1883, and 1st Clerk 1889; pensioned 1901. Recorded as receiving the Hessian General Medal of Honour (Silver) 'For Merit' Ludwig III, 25 June 1891.

81 Mr Arthur Frank Feltham

1889. Presented by Queen Victoria to Mr Arthur Frank Feltham, First Master Cook, for faithful services to the Queen during 30 years.

Born Dover, about 1844. Entered service of Queen Victoria in June 1859 as an

Apprentice in the Kitchen; Assistant Cook 1864, Yeoman of the Kitchen 1868 until 1871; not listed in the Imperial Calendar again until 1881 when he appears as Fourth Master Cook, Third Master Cook 1882, Second Master Cook 1888, and First Master Cook 1889; became Chief Cook in 1892 and retired in 1897. Recorded as receiving the Hessian Medal of Merit (Bronze), bearing the head of the Grand Duchess Alice on 25 June 1891.

82 Mr George Frederick Malsch

1889. Presented by Queen Victoria to Mr George Frederick Malsch, Second Master Cook, for faithful services to the Queen during 33 years. One Bar for service.

Entered service of Queen Victoria in October 1856 as an Apprentice in the Kitchen; was engaged as Cook to the Prince of Wales when at Cambridge in 1861, and re-entered HM's service as 3rd Assistant Cook 1863; listed in this capacity first in the 1865 Imperial Calendar, promoted 2nd Assistant Cook 1866, and 1st Assistant Cook 1870; became 2nd Yeoman of the Kitchen 1877, and 1st Yeoman in 1881; 4th Master Cook 1882, 3rd 1888, 2nd 1889, and finally

GEORGE MALSCH

promoted 1st Master Cook in 1892; pensioned 1901.

83 Mr Alexander Grant

1889. Presented by Queen Victoria to Mr Alexander Grant, Messenger, for faithful services to the Queen and her son, Prince Leopold, during 24 years.
One Bar for service.

The second son of John Grant (No. 15 above), Keeper at Balmoral. Entered the service of Queen Victoria on 10 September

EDWARD LAWLEY

ALEXANDER GRANT

1865 in the Steward's Room; entered service of Prince Leopold, Duke of Albany, 17 February 1867, as Wardrobe Man, and in 1884 on the death of Prince Leopold became Messenger to the Queen; pensioned 1901. Recorded as receiving the Hessian General Medal of Honour (Silver) 'For Merit' Ludwig III 8 September 1883.

84 Muhammad Bakhsh

1889. Presented by the Queen Empress Victoria to Muhammad Bakhsh in recognition of his faithful services to Her Majesty.

Muhammad Bakhsh and Abdul Karim were the first of Queen Victoria's Indian Attendants and entered her service in July 1887. Bakhsh had formerly been in the service of Major General Sir Thomas Dennehy, formerly Political Agent in Rajputana, who became an Extra Groom in Waiting to Queen Victoria in 1888. Bakhsh's Medal was struck and named for presentation within a week as he was supposed to be returning to India imminently; however, his name appears in the Imperial Calendar until 1891.

MUHAMMAD BAKHSH

85 Mr William Wilkins

1890. Presented by Queen Victoria to Mr William Wilkins, First Gentleman Porter, for faithful services to the Queen during 31 years.

Born 1836. Entered service of Queen Victoria in 1859; first listed in the Imperial Calendar as Assistant Gentleman Porter 1873; Groom Porter 1876, 2nd Yeoman Gentleman Porter 1878, 1st Yeoman Gentleman Porter 1887; Principal Gentleman Porter 1889. Died 15 December 1891 at 9 Albany Terrace, Windsor. Recorded as receiving the Hessian Medal of Merit (Bronze), bearing the head of the Grand Duchess Alice July1887.

WILLIAM BLANE

86 Mr William Jonathan Blane

1890. Presented by Queen Victoria to Mr William Jonathan Blane, Second Clerk of the Kitchen, for faithful services to the Queen during 29 years.

One Bar for service.

Born 1836. Entered service of Queen Victoria 3 February 1861 as Footman; 3rd Clerk of the Kitchen 1883 and 2nd Clerk 1890; he was retained in Edward VII's service after the death of Queen

Victoria, and was made Principal Gentleman Porter in 1902; retired 1910. Died 13 November 1915 at 1 Balmoral Villas, New Road, Windsor. Recipient of 1887 Jubilee Medal in Silver, with 1897 Bar, Coronation Medal 1902 (Bronze), Prussia – Medal of the Order of the Red Eagle (Silver), Norway – Haakon VII King's Commemoration Medal (Gold, small size with crown), Spain – Order of Naval Merit 5th Class June 1905, Italy – Victor Emanuel III Royal Service Medal (Gold) November 1903, Portugal – Carlos 1st Coronation Medal 1889 (Silver) November 1904, Sweden – Gustav V Royal Household Medal (Gilt, with crown, small size), and Württemberg – William II Medal of Merit (Silver) 10 February 1904. Blane also had the RVM Edward VII (Silver) 2 August 1910. Married to Mary Grace, née Meredith, sister of John Meredith (No. 127 below).

87 Mr Frederick Moneyment Walker

1890. Presented by Queen Victoria to Mr Frederick Moneyment Walker, Yeoman of the Cellars, for faithful services to the Queen during 27 years.

One Bar for service.

Born 1849. Entered service of Queen Victoria 1863; first listed in the Imperial Calendar as Groom of the Wine Cellars 1869, 2nd Yeoman 1884, 1st Yeoman 1890; not listed 1894–1901; King's Messenger 1902–16. Walker was a Groom of the Great Chamber 1892–95. RVM 9 (Silver) 1 August 1910. Recorded as receiving Hessian General Medal of Honour Ludwig III (Silver) 25 June 1891. Died 12 July 1923 at 86 Calbourne Road, Balham, and buried in Windsor Cemetery. Refs.: *Windsor & Eton Express*, 20 July 1923.

88 Mr Thomas Smith

1890. Presented by Queen Victoria to Mr Thomas Smith, Messenger, for faithful services to the Queen during 23 years.

One Bar for service.

Entered service of Queen Victoria 1867 as an Extra Assistant in the Wine Cellars; 2nd Yeoman of the Wine Cellars 1875, and 1st Yeoman 1884; appointed Messenger to the Queen 1890; pensioned 1901.

89 Syad Ahmad Husain

1891. Presented by the Queen Empress Victoria to Syad Ahmad Husain, in recognition of his faithful services to Her Majesty.

First listed in the Imperial Calendar in 1889, no longer listed 1892. Recorded as receiving the Hessian Medal of Merit (Bronze), bearing the head of the Grand Duke Ludwig IV on the occasion of the Queen's visit to Darmstadt 25 April 1890.

90 Mr George Woodford

1891. Presented by Queen Victoria to Mr George Woodford, Tapissier at Osborne, for faithful services to the Queen during 35 years.

Born 1834. Entered service of Queen Victoria in 1856; retired as Tapissier at Osborne July 1903 when he was presented with the RVM (Silver) by Edward VII. Died on 14 October 1914 at Corbiere, West Hill, St Helens, Isle of Wight. Refs.: *The Times*, 17 October 1914.

91 Mr Joseph William Bailey

1891. Presented by Queen Victoria to Mr Joseph William Bailey, Gentleman Porter, for faithful services to the Queen during 33 years.

Born 1840. Entered service of the Duchess of Kent 1857, and that of the Queen 1858; Assistant Table Decker 1859, Wax Fitter 1866, Third Table Decker 1878; promoted

THOMAS SMITH

Assistant Porter 1885, Groom Porter 1887, Yeoman Gentleman Porter 1893, and 1st Yeoman of the Silver Pantry 1894; retired 1903. Died 31 March 1915 at Malden House, Francis Road, Windsor, buried Windsor Cemetery. Refs.: *Windsor & Eton Express*, 10 April 1915.

GEORGE SPEARING

92 Mr George Farley Spearing

1891. Presented by Queen Victoria to Mr George Farley Spearing, Gentleman Porter, for faithful services to the Queen during 32 years.

Born 1833. Entered service of Queen Victoria as Footman in 1859; promoted Livery Porter at Buckingham Palace 1867; Assistant Gentleman Porter 1888, Groom Porter 1889, Yeoman Gentleman Porter 1894; pensioned 1901. Died 23 November 1904 at Farley Villa, Balfour Road, Wimbledon.

93 Andrew Thomson, Esq.

1891. Presented by Queen Victoria to Andrew Thomson, Esq., Page of the Presence, for faithful services to the Queen during 25 years.

Born 1835. Entered service of Queen Victoria in 1866; first listed in the Imperial Calendar as Assistant Gentleman Porter

ANDREW THOMSON

1887, Groom Porter 1888, Page of the Presence 1890; pensioned 1901. Died 22 March 1906 at 10 Lessar Avenue, Clapham. He was an elder brother of Charles Thomson (No. 77 above).

94 Francis Orchard, Esq.

1891. Presented by Queen Victoria to Francis Orchard, Esq., Page of the Presence, for faithful services to the Queen during 25 years.

FRANCIS ORCHARD

Born 1843. Entered the service of Queen Victoria in July 1866 as Footman; Page of the Presence 1887, and Page of the Backstairs 1899; Page of the Backstairs to Edward VII; pensioned at Christmas 1901. Died 23 April 1904 at 'Lauderdale', King's Road, Windsor, buried in Windsor Cemetery where there is a headstone. He received the RVM from Edward VII April 1901, and was also the recipient of the 1887 Jubilee Medal (Silver) with bar 1897, Denmark Christian IX Royal Household Medal (Gold with crown), Siam Chulalongkorn Rajaruchi Medal 5th Reign (Silver); and was a beneficiary in the will of Queen Victoria, receiving a legacy of £30. Refs.: *Windsor & Eton Express*, 27 April and 11 May 1901, and 30 April 1904.

95 Mr Francis Clark

1891. Presented by Queen Victoria to Mr Francis Clark, Highland Attendant, for faithful services to the Queen during 21 years.

Born at Belmore, Aberdarder, 1 September 1841. Entered service of Queen Victoria as Highland Attendant 1870. Died 7 July 1895 at Buckingham Palace, and buried at Braemar. He was a nephew of John Brown, and shared the duties of Highland Attendant with Hugh Brown, another brother of John Brown. From a photograph in his Highland dress he wears, apart from his Faithful Service Medal, the 1887 Jubilee Medal (Silver),

FRANCIS CLARK

the Medal of the Order of the Red Eagle (?), Hesse – Medal of Merit (Bronze), bearing the head of the Grand Duchess Alice on the occasion of the Queen's visit to Darmstadt 25 April 1890. There is a memorial to him in Crathie Churchyard erected by Queen Victoria. Refs.: *Black and White*, 13 July 1895.

MISS EMILIE DITTWEILER

96 Miss Emilie Dittweiler

1892. Presented by Queen Victoria to Miss Emilie Dittweiler, Dresser to Her Majesty, for faithful services to the Queen during 33 years.

Born about 1831. A native of Carlsruhe in the Grand Duchy of Baden. Entered service of Queen Victoria as Dresser in October 1859 and retired in 1892. Died at Carlsruhe 9 March 1899. Recorded as receiving the Hessian Medal of Merit (Bronze) bearing the head of the Grand Duchess Alice July 1887. Refs.: *The Times*, 13 March 1899.

97 Mrs Annie Macdonald

1892. Presented by Queen Victoria to Mrs. Annie Macdonald, Wardrobe Woman to Her Majesty, for faithful services to the Queen during 38 years.

Born 3 January 1832 at Carnna Cuinhne, the daughter of William Mitchel, the blacksmith at Clachanturn, near Abergeldie. Entered service of Queen Victoria in 1854.

Married John Alexander McDonald, a Footman in the Queen's service and who died of consumption 1 October 1865, aged 37. Mrs Macdonald died at Clachanturn 4 July 1897, buried at Crathie. Refs.: *The Times*, 6 and 10 July 1897.

98 Hadji Mirza Yusuf Beg

1892. Presented by the Queen Empress Victoria to Hadji Mirza Yusuf Beg, in recognition of his faithful services to Her Majesty.

He is first and last listed in the Imperial Calendar of 1892, and appears only to have served one year in the Queen's service. Recorded as receiving the Hessian Medal of Merit (Bronze), bearing the head of the Grand Duke Ludwig IV, January 1892.

99 Mr George Carver

1892. Presented by Queen Victoria to Mr George Carver, Lamplighter, for faithful services to the Queen during 38 years.

Entered service of Queen Victoria as Assistant Lamplighter 1854; 2nd Lamplighter 1881, 1st Lamplighter 1886; retired 1894.

100 John Heir, Esq.

1892. Presented by Queen Victoria to John Heir, Esq., Page of the Presence, for faithful services to the Queen during 28 years.

Born 1846. Entered service of Queen Victoria 1864 as Footman; Page of the Presence 1888; pensioned 1901. Died 15 March 1925 at 18 Albany Road, Windsor, and buried in Windsor Cemetery. Recipient of 1887 Jubilee Medal (Silver) and 1897 bar, and Siam – King Chulalongkorn Rajaruchi Medal 5th Reign (Silver). Refs.: *Windsor & Eton Express*, 27 March 1925. Related to No. 76.

101 Mr Charles Hughes

1892. Presented by Queen Victoria to Mr Charles Hughes, Marshalman, for faithful services to the Queen during 40 years.

Born about 1838. Entered service of Queen Victoria in 1852 as Assistant in the Steward's Room; attached to the Royal Nursery from 1862; Page's man 1871, and made a Marshalman 1888. Died 19 October 1896.

THE VICTORIA FAITHFUL SERVICE MEDAL · 53

JOHN MANNING

102 John Manning, Esq.

1892. Presented by Queen Victoria to John Manning, Esq., Superintendent, Royal Mews, Windsor, for faithful services to the Queen during 48 years.

Entered service of Queen Victoria 2 November 1844 as a Weekly Helper, appointed Established Helper 8 April 1870 and Superintendent of the Royal Mews at Windsor 23 February 1884. Retired on pension 30 July 1896 aged 67. Was a recipient of Queen Victoria's Jubilee medal 1887 (Silver).

JOHN HEIR

103 Mr Frederick Elmer

1892. Presented by Queen Victoria to Mr Frederick Elmer, Groom, for faithful services to the Queen during 30 years.

Born in Newmarket about 1837. Entered service of Queen Victoria 1862 as a Groom in the Royal Mews. Of 35 Mysore Road, Lavender Hill, Surrey. Died 17 October 1910 at the London County Asylum, Banstead, and buried in Wandsworth Cemetery. Refs.: *Windsor & Eton Express*, 22 October 1910.

FREDERICK ELMER

104 Ahmed Khan

1893. Presented by the Queen Empress Victoria to Ahmed Khan, in recognition of his faithful services to Her Majesty.

Entered service of Queen Victoria 1891; listed in the Imperial Calendar 1893–9.

105 Mr Isaac Rayner

1893. Presented by Queen Victoria to Mr Isaac Rayner, Marshalman, for faithful services to the Queen during 52 years.

Entered service of Queen Victoria 1841; first listed in the Imperial Calendar as a Coal Porter 1847, Messenger Clerk of the Kitchen's Office 1854, and made a Marshalman 1880; last listed 1900.

106 Mr Josiah Miles

1893. Presented by Queen Victoria to Mr Josiah Miles, Stud Groom, for faithful services to the Queen during 49 years.

Born about 1814. Entered service of Queen Victoria 1844. Died at Cumberland Lodge, Windsor Great Park, 22 March 1894, and buried in Highgate Cemetery. Refs.: *Windsor & Eton Express*, 31 March 1894.

107 Mr George Shorter

1893. Presented by Queen Victoria to Mr George Shorter, Sergeant Footman, for faithful services to the Queen during 26 years.

Born 20 September 1844 at Bromley, Kent. Entered service of Queen Victoria as Footman 6 December 1867; Sergeant Footman 1892, Groom Porter 1895, and a Page of the Presence in 1898; Page of the Backstairs to King Edward VII 1902, State Page 1907; retired 1915. Died 10 March 1918 at 17 Trinity Place, Windsor, was the recipient of 13 other medals: RVM Edward VII (Silver) 2 August 1910, 1887 Jubilee Medal (Silver) with 1897 bar, 1902 Coronation Medal (Bronze), 1911 Coronation Medal, Prussia – General Decoration of Honour in January 1901 on German Emperor's Visit to Osborne and Windsor, Italy – Victor Emanuel III Royal Service Medal (Gold) 6 November 1903 on King and Queen of Italy's visit to Windsor, Prussia – Medal of the Order of the Crown (Gilt) on German Emperor's visit to Osborne 1889, Prussia – Medal of the Order of the Red Eagle (Silver) on German Emperor's Visit to Windsor, November 1899, Bulgaria – Cross of Merit of the Order of St. Alexander, 11 March 1905 when Prince of Bulgaria visited Buckingham Palace, Portugal – Carlos 1st Coronation Medal 1889

GEORGE SHORTER

(Silver) November 1904 when King and Queen of Portugal at Windsor, Rumania – Medal of Merit (Silver) 1 November 1892 when Queen of Rumania at Balmoral, Hesse – Ludwig IV Medal for Merit (large Bronze) 25 April 1890 during the Queen's visit to Darmstadt, Saxe-Coburg – Medal of Merit of the Ducal Saxe-Ernestine House Order bearing the head of Ernest II (Silver) April 1894 during the Queen's visit to Coburg from Alfred Duke of Coburg. Two sons were in the Royal service: Frederick who became 1st Yeoman of the Wine Cellars (see George V FSM) and Arthur who subsequently became Chef to the Governor-General of Canada.

108 Mr William Slark

1893. Presented by Queen Victoria to Mr William Slark, Postillion, for faithful services to the Queen during 33 years.

Born 1846 in Royal Mews, Pimlico. Entered service of Queen Victoria 1860 as a Groom, later to become a Postillion and Queen's Postillion, retiring in 1893. Died 2 February 1915 at 23 Upton Park Road, Forest Gate, Essex; buried in Teddington Cemetery. Both his father and grandfather were in Royal Service. Refs.: *Windsor & Eton Express*, 6 February 1915.

109 Mr James Hutchinson

1893. Presented by Queen Victoria to Mr James Hutchinson, Coachman, for faithful services to the Queen during 29 years.

Born 24 December 1842 at Braemar. Entered service of Queen Victoria 1864 as a Groom, subsequently Coachman. Died 22 October 1910 at 53 Queens Road, New Windsor, and buried in Windsor Cemetery.

110 Mr Goss Overton

1893. Presented by Queen Victoria to Mr Goss Overton, Keeper, Windsor Great Park, for faithful services to the Queen during 24 years.

Born 16 December 1835. Entered service of Albert Edward Prince of Wales as Game Keeper at Sandringham 1864; transferred to Windsor Great Park as Head Keeper 1870; retired 23 March 1906. Died 15 December 1914 at Gosford

GOSS OVERTON

House, 68 Longley Road, Tooting, Surrey, and buried in Cranbourne Churchyard, Windsor Great Park. Also had 1887 Jubilee Medal (Silver) and 1897 bar, 1902 Coronation Medal (Silver), Prussia – Medal of the Order of the Red Eagle (Silver), Italy – Order of the Crown 5th Class, November 1903 on King and Queen of Italy's Visit to Windsor Castle, Portugal – Order of Villa Vicosa 4th Class, December 1902 on King and Queen of Portugal's visit to Windsor Castle, Saxe-Coburg – Cross of Merit of the Ducal Saxe-Ernestine House Order (Silver) also National Thanksgiving Medallion for the Recovery of the Prince of Wales 1872 (Silver). Overton is mentioned on several occasions in the *Windsor & Eton Express* accompanying Royal Shooting Parties – 22 November

JAMES HUTCHINSON

and 13 December 1902, 21 and 28 November 1903, 19 November 1904, 18 November 1905, 31 March 1906 (retirement).

111 Mr Samuel Ponder

1894. Presented by Queen Victoria to Mr Samuel Ponder, 1st Yeoman of the Confectionery, for faithful services to the Queen during 25 years.

Born Westminster 1833. Entered service of Queen Victoria 1869; listed in the Imperial Calendar 1870–1901.

SAMUEL PONDER

112 Mr John Brown Seymour

1894. Presented by Queen Victoria to Mr John Brown Seymour, Tapissier, for faithful services to the Queen during 38 years.

Born 1829. Entered service of Queen Victoria in 1856 on the Inspection Staff at Windsor Castle; in the Packing Room at Windsor Castle from 1 July 1870, and Travelling Tapissier to the Queen; he was assisted by his brother Thomas Seymour; Both received RVM of Queen Victoria in February 1901: John Seymour in Silver, Thomas in Bronze. John was pensioned 1910. Groom of the Great Chamber from 1906. Died at 23 Wellington Street, Slough, 1 December 1915, buried in Slough Parish Churchyard. His brother predeceased him three days previously on 29 November 1915 and was also buried at Slough. J. B. Seymour is recorded as receiving the Hessian Medal of Merit (Bronze), bearing the head of the Grand

JOHN SEYMOUR

Duchess Alice on the occasion of the Queen's visit to Darmstadt 25 April 1890; the Silver Cross of the Hessian Order of Philip 8 July 1895; he also had the Saxe-Coburg Merit Medal of Saxe-Ernestine House Order bearing the head of Ernest II at a date not known. See *Windsor & Eton Express*, 4 and 11 December 1915.

113 Mr Frederick Green Vaughan

1894. Presented by Queen Victoria to Mr Frederick Green Vaughan, Private Bookbinder, for faithful services to the Queen during 34 years.

FREDERICK VAUGHAN

Born 1837. Entered service of Queen Victoria as an Assistant in the Steward's Room 1861; Waiter in the Royal Nursery 1864; Assistant Table Decker 1866 until 1873 at which time he is no longer listed in the Imperial Calendar, and became Bookbinder; RVM of Queen Victoria (Silver) February 1901; also received 1902 and 1911 Coronation Medals. Died 10 June 1914 at Guy's Hospital, London, and buried in Morden Cemetery; at the time of his death living at Hillesley, Glos. His son Frank succeeded him as Bookbinder; MVO (V) 5 July 1939, retired 1 October 1939; died 11 February 1960.

114 Mr John Kennedy

1894 Presented by Queen Victoria to Mr John Kennedy, Yeoman of the Stewards' Room, for faithful services to the Queen during 34 years.

Born 1832. Entered service of Queen Victoria in 1860 as a Night Porter; Pages Man 1866, promoted Yeoman of the Stewards' Room 1880; died in service 19 May 1897 at 1 Albion Place, Alma Road, Clewer, Windsor, and buried in Windsor Cemetery. Two of his sons were in Royal service: John Arthur Kennedy and Ralph Kennedy (see George V Register below). Refs.: *Windsor & Eton Express*, 22 and 29 May 1897.

115 Mr John McLean

1894. Presented by Queen Victoria to Mr John McLean, Messenger to Robes Office, for faithful services to the Queen during 35 years.

Born about 1826. Entered service of Queen Victoria 1859. Died 3 September 1898 at 32 Sarsfield Road, Balham, Surrey.

116 William Henderson, Esq.

1895. Presented by Queen Victoria to William Henderson, Esq., Page, for faithful services to the Queen during 26 years.

Born Clapton, Middlesex about 1848. Entered service of Queen Victoria in 1869 as Footman; Page of the Presence 1892; retired 1897.

117 Mr Frederick Brown

1895. Presented by Queen Victoria to Mr Frederick Brown, Marshalman, for faithful services to the Queen during 54 years.

Entered service of Queen Victoria in 1841 as an Assistant in the Coal Yard; Green Office Man in April 1843, made Marshalman June 1887: last listed in Imperial Calendar 1900.

118 Mr Daniel Rayner

1895. Presented by Queen Victoria to Mr Daniel Rayner, Under State Porter, for faithful services to the Queen during 51 years.

Born in about 1819 at Stisted, Essex. Entered service of Queen Victoria 1844 in the Coal Yard; became Nursery Waiter October 1850, and promoted to Under State Porter February 1863; last listed in Imperial Calendar 1896. Died 17 December 1898 at 12 Haldane Road, Fulham, Middlesex.

119 Mr Edwin Miller

1895. Presented by Queen Victoria to Mr Edwin Miller, State Coachman, for faithful service to the Queen during 36 years.

Entered service of Queen Victoria 8 February 1859; first listed in Royal Kalendar as Coachman 1887, and Imperial Calendar as State Coachman 1891; retired 1898. Recipient of 1887 Jubilee Medal (Silver) and 1897 bar, Prussia – Medal of the Order of the

WILLIAM HENDERSON

EDWIN MILLER

Crown (Gilt) Wilhelm II, and Siam – King Chulalongkorn Rajaruchi Medal 5th Reign (Silver). Refs. *The Sketch*, 23 October 1895.

120 Charles Taylor, Esq.

1896. Presented by Queen Victoria to Charles Taylor, Esq., Inspector at Buckingham Palace, for faithful services to the Queen during 38 years.

Born 23 July 1836. Entered service of Queen Victoria in 1858 as Joiner at Buckingham Palace; appointed Tapissier at the Royal Pavilion, Aldershot, and later at Buckingham Palace 1888, and Holyrood 1891; Inspector at Buckingham Palace 1894; MVO (V) 30 December 1904, retired in 1906. Died 19 February 1908 at 54 Bradbourne Street, Fulham. Was also recipient of the 1887 Jubilee (Silver) with 1897 bar, 1902 Coronation (Silver), Siam – King Chulalongkorn Rajaruchi Medal 5th Reign (Silver) on the occasion of the King's visit to England on 30 July 1897.

121 Mr Henry Bryant

1896. Presented by Queen Victoria to Mr Henry Bryant, Yeoman of the Silver Pantry, for faithful services to the Queen during 29 years.

Born 1845. Entered service of Queen Victoria in 1867; first listed in Imperial Calendar as Coal Porter 1873, Assistant in the Silver Pantry 1876, Under Butler 1878, Yeoman of the Silver Pantry 1883; pensioned July 1922. Living at 21 St Leonard's Avenue, Windsor, he died at his daughter's home in Steyning, Sussex, 1 July 1923. Buried in Windsor Cemetery. Recipient of RVM Edward VII (Silver) 2 August 1910. See *Windsor & Eton Express*, 6 & 13 July 1923.

122 Mr C. Burbidge

1896. Presented by Queen Victoria to Mr C. Burbidge, Marshalman, for faithful services to the Queen during 52 years.

Born 1821, Charles Burbidge entered service of Queen Victoria in 1844; first listed in the Imperial Calendar as Steam Apparatus Man in the Royal Kitchens 1847, Scourer 1854, made Marshalman 1881. Died 31 March 1896 at 8 Bullen Street, Battersea.

123 Mr Isaac Ridgeon

1896. Presented by Queen Victoria to Mr Isaac Ridgeon, State Porter, for faithful services to the Queen during 50 years.

Born about 1825. Entered the service of Queen Victoria in 1846; first listed in the Imperial Calendar as 2nd Assistant in Servants' Hall 1853, 1st Assistant 1861, Errand Man in the Kitchen 1868; Under State Porter 1880, Yeoman State Porter 1893; pensioned 1901. Died 24 October 1919 at 25 Glebe Road. Hornsey, Middx., and buried in Clewer Churchyard, Windsor.

Mr Alexander Francis Mackenzie

1896. Presented by Queen Victoria to Mr Alexander Francis Mackenzie, Second Table Decker, for faithful services to the Queen during 25 years.

Entered service of Queen Victoria in 1871; first listed in Imperial Calendar as 2nd Table Decker 1872; last listed 1900. Though an order was given for a Medal for Mackenzie on 3 June 1896, it is not certain whether he was given it; his name does not appear in any printed register.

HENRY MANNING

124 Mr Henry Arthur Manning

1898. Presented by Queen Victoria to Mr Henry Arthur Manning. Second Master Cook, for faithful services to the Queen during 29 years.

Born 1854. Entered service of Queen Victoria as an Apprentice in the Kitchen 1869; Assistant Cook 1876, 2nd Yeoman of the Kitchen 1881, 1st Yeoman 1882, 4th Master Cook 1888, 3rd Master Cook 1889, 2nd Master Cook 1892; pensioned 1901. Died 21 July 1913 at 1 Dorset Road, Windsor, and cremated at Woking Crematorium. Also recipient of 1887 Jubilee Medal (Silver) with 1897 bar, and Siam – King Chulalongkorn Rajaaruchi Medal 5th Reign (Silver) on the King's visit 30 July 1897. Refs.: *Windsor & Eton Express*, 26 July 1913.

125 Mr William George Robinson

1898. Presented by Queen Victoria to Mr William George Robinson, State Yeoman Porter, for faithful services to the Queen during 39 years.

Entered service of Queen Victoria in 1859 as Under State Porter; Yeoman State Porter 1887; retired 1906 .

126 Mr Frederick Lowes

1898. Presented by Queen Victoria to Mr Frederick Lowes, Groom Porter, for faithful services to the Queen during 29 years.

Born 1841. Entered service of Queen Victoria on 1 November 1869 as Footman; listed in the Royal Kalendar in the Department of the Master of the Horse as Porter 1887; Assistant Groom Porter 1894, Gentleman Porter 1902, Principal Gentleman Porter 1911. Died in service on 9 April 1918 at 2 Consort Villas, Arthur Road, Clewer, Windsor; buried at Clewer Churchyard. Recipient of RVM Edward VII (Silver) 2 August 1910, 1887 Jubilee Medal (Silver) with Bar 1897, 1902 Coronation Medal (Bronze), 1911 Coronation Medal, and the following foreign awards : Denmark – Christian X King's Medal of Recompense (Gilt) 14 May 1914, Prussia – William II Medal of the Order of the Red Eagle (Gilt) November 1907, Sweden – Gustav V Royal Household Medal (Gilt) small size, November 1908, France – Medal of Honour Ministry of Foreign Affairs (Silver) President Poincaré 15 July 1913, Servia – Royal Service Medal (Gilt) May 1911, Spain – Alphonso XIII Order of Naval Merit 5th Class, November 1907, Portugal – Carlos 1st Coronation Medal 1889 (Silver) November 1904, Siam–Chulalongkorn Rajaruchi Medal 5th Reign (Silver) 30 July 1897. Refs.: *Windsor & Eton Express*, 4 & 11 May 1918; *The Times*, 3 May 1918.

127 John Meredith, Esq.

1898. Presented by Queen Victoria to Mr John Meredith, Page of the Presence, for faithful services to the Queen during 22 years.

Born 15 April 1854 in the Royal Mews, Pimlico. Entered service of Queen Victoria as Footman 1876; Groom Porter 1895; Page of the Presence 1898; was retained by Edward VII and appointed a Page of the Backstairs to George V 7 May 1910; appointed a State Page 1 February 1915. Died at 1 Lancaster Villas, New Road, Clewer, Windsor, 21 June 1926. Meredith's father, James, was also in service with Queen Victoria: born 27 December 1827, entered the Queen's service as Footman 1854, 2nd Yeoman of the Wine and Beer Cellars 27 February 1858, 1st Yeoman 1867, State Page 1875, and died 27 January 1876. John Meredith received the RVM Edward VII (Silver) 13 August 1910, 1887 Jubilee Medal (Silver)

JOHN MEREDITH

and 1897 bar, 1902 (Bronze) and 1911 Coronation Medals; also Russia – Nicholas II Medal for Zeal (Gold) worn from the St Stanislas ribbon, Prussia – Medal of the Order of the Crown (Gilt), Prussia – Medal of the Order of the Red Eagle (Silver), Norway – Haakon VII King's Commemoration Medal (Gold with Crown), Denmark – Frederick VIII King's Medal of Recompense (Gilt), Sweden – Medal of the Order of the Vasa (Gilt, small size), Montenegro – Prince Nicholas 1st Medal for Ipal (Gilt), Italy – Royal Service Medal Victor Emanuel III (Silver), Portugal – Carlos 1st Coronation Medal 1889 (Silver), Saxe-Coburg – Medal of Merit of the Ducal Saxe-Ernestine House Order (Silver), bearing the head of Ernest II, Baden – Grand Duke Frederick Medal for Merit (Silver).

128 Shekh Ghulam Mustafa

1898. Presented by the Queen Empress Victoria to Shekh Ghulam Mustafa in recognition of his faithful services to Her Majesty.

Entered service as Cook to Munshi Abdul Karim 1 April 1890, later becoming Indian Attendant to the Queen; listed as

such in the Imperial Calendar from 1892 to 1898. In a photograph taken at the time of Queen Victoria's 1897 Jubilee, he wears the following awards: RVM Victoria (Silver) August 1896, (duplicate was given in February 1901) Saxe-Coburg – Medal of Merit of the Ducal Saxe-Ernestine House Order, bearing the head of Ernest II, Hesse – General Medal of Honour Ludwig IV, – 'for Merit' (29 April 1895) Prussia – Medal of the Order of the Red Eagle, and another unidentified award.

129 Mr William Woods

1899. Presented by Queen Victoria to Mr William Woods, Gate Porter at Windsor, for faithful services to the Queen during 47 years.

Born about 1833 at Newmarket. Entered the service of Queen Victoria 1852. Formerly a Coachman. Died 13 November 1910 at Wood Villa, Wellington Road, Slough.

SHEKH MUSTAFA (*left*) AND SHEKH CHIDDA (*right*) WITH QUEEN VICTORIA

130 Mr George Woods

1899. Presented by Queen Victoria to Mr George Woods, Coachman, for faithful services to the Queen during 40 years.

Born in 1837 at Docking, Norfolk. Entered the service of Queen Victoria in 1859. Died 14 April 1906 at 22 Adelaide Square, Windsor, and buried in Clewer Churchyard. Refs.: *Windsor & Eton Express*, 21 April 1906.

131 Mr William Oakes

1899. Presented by Queen Victoria to Mr William Oakes, Coachman, for faithful services to the Queen during 39 years.

Born in Pimlico in 1848. Entered the service of Queen Victoria 19 October 1859 as a Groom; Third Class Helper (Postillion) 1880, Second Class Helper (Coachman) 1 January 1887, (Acting Coachman 1886), 1st Class Coachman. 1 October 1893; retired 1903–04. Died 31 January 1922 at 91 New Kings Road, Fulham, Middx. Recipient also of 1887 Jubilee Medal (Bronze) and 1897 bar, and 1902 Coronation Medal (Bronze).

132 Mr John Ashforth

1899. Presented by Queen Victoria to Mr John Ashforth, Lamplighter, for faithful service to the Queen during 34 years.

Entered service of Queen Victoria in 1865 as an Assistant Lamplighter; promoted 2nd Lamplighter 1887, and 1st Lamplighter 1895; pensioned 1901.

133 Mr Alfred Wilkins

1899. Presented by Queen Victoria to Mr Alfred Wilkins, Yeoman of the Steward's Room, for faithful services to the Queen during 28 years.

Entered service of Queen Victoria in 1871 as Assistant in Steward's Room; Pages man 1886, Yeoman of the Steward's Room 1898; pensioned 1901.

134 Mr George Bullen

1899. Presented by Queen Victoria to Mr George Bullen, Established Helper, for faithful services to the Queen during 28 years.

Born in 1858. Entered service of Queen Victoria on 23 December 1871; promoted to Established Helper 1 October 1893, and listed in the Imperial Calendar as an Outrider from 1895.

135 Miss Elizabeth Stewart

1899. Presented by Queen Victoria to Miss Elizabeth Stewart, Wardrobe Woman, for faithful services to the Queen during 29 years.

Medal engraved without 'Miss' on it. Born 1 April 1848, the daughter of Alexander and Mary Stewart, née Michie, of Toldhu Farm, Glenmuick, near Ballater, Aberdeenshire. Entered the service of Queen Victoria as a Housemaid at Balmoral 1868; Wardrobe Woman to the Queen 1879. Received 1887 Jubilee Medal (Bronze) and in 1897 a Silver 1887 Medal with 1897 bar (Silver). Pensioned 1901 when she went to live with her brother, John Stewart, who rented the Toldhu Farm, Glenmuick, near Ballater; John Stewart gave up the farm in 1913 and he and his sister went to live at Windsor Cottage, Ballater. Elizabeth Stewart died 20 March 1919 at the Royal Asylum, Aberdeen, and is buried in the Churchyard at Crathie. Refs.: *More Leaves from a Journal of a Life in the Highlands*; *The Weekly Free Press* and *Aberdeen Herald*, 29 March 1919.

136 Mr Samuel McKenzie Hammond

1900. Presented by Queen Victoria to Mr Samuel McKenzie Hammond, Keeper of the Royal Apartments on the Royal Yacht, for faithful services to the Queen during 23 years.

Born on 5 November 1858. Entered service of Queen Victoria as Steward in the Royal Yacht *Victoria and Albert* 19 December 1877; made Keeper of the Royal Apartments from 1881; retired on 9 March 1932. Died 12 December 1932. A full list of Hammond's many awards is not available, but he is known to have had the following: MVO (V) given 3 June 1931, RVM Edward VII (Silver) 28 April 1905, Victoria Faithful Service Medal, 1887 Jubilee Medal (Silver) with 1897 bar, 1902 Coronation Medal (Bronze), 1911 Coronation Medal, Naval L.S. & G.C Medal, British War Medal 1914–1918, Norway – Haakon VII

Coronation Medal 1906 (Silver). Refs.: *The Times*, 14 and 20 December 1932; *The Evening News of Portsmouth*, 14 and 20 December 1932; *Hants. Telegraph and Post* & *The Naval Chronicle*, 16 December 1932.

THOMAS BEAUMONT

137 Mr Thomas Beaumont

1900. Presented by Queen Victoria to Mr Thomas Beaumont, Established Helper, for faithful services to the Queen during 35 years.

Born in 1841 at Fulbourne, Cambs. Entered service of Queen Victoria in 1845; pensioned 1900.

138 Mr William Boswell

1900. Presented by Queen Victoria to Mr William Boswell, Sergeant Footman, for faithful services to the Queen and Prince and Princess Christian of Schleswig-Holstein during 21 years.

Born in 1859. Entered service of Prince and Princess Christian 1879 and the Queen's service 23 May 1884, Sergeant Footman 1895, Page of the Presence 1902,

Page of the Backstairs 1904; Steward to Queen Alexandra 1911; pensioned on the death of Queen Alexandra 1925. Died 10 March 1934 at Jackson's Cottage, Sandringham, and buried at Sandringham.

139 Mr George Hiley

1900. Presented by Queen Victoria to Mr George Hiley, Established Helper, for faithful services to the Queen during 45 years.

Born in Brighton about 1836. Entered service of Queen Victoria 1855. Died 6 June 1908 at 9 Victoria Street, Windsor, and buried in Windsor Cemetery.

Mr Alexander Rankin

1900. Presented by Queen Victoria to Mr Alexander Rankin, Highland Attendant for faithful services to the Queen during 19 years.

Entered service of Queen Victoria as Highland Servant on 14 April 1881; promoted to Highland Attendant 1895; last listed 1900. Medal given 11 September 1900.

ALEXANDER RANKIN

Mr George Gordon

1900. Presented by Queen Victoria to Mr George Gordon of Dalraddie for faithful services to the Queen during 32 years.

Medal given 10 November 1900.

Shekh Chidda

1900. Presented by the Queen Empress Victoria to Shekh Chidda in recognition of his faithful services to Her Majesty.

Medal given 17 November 1900.

SHEKH CHIDDA

Mr John Michie

1901. Presented by Queen Victoria to Mr John Michie, Forester at Balmoral, for faithful services to the Queen during 20 years.

Born on 8 June 1853, son of D. K. Michie of Redfield. Educated at Perth Academy. Entered service of Queen Victoria at Balmoral on 13 August 1880 as forester; Factor to King Edward VII at Balmoral 1902; MVO (V) 9 November 1903 and promoted to MVO (IV) 5 July 1919 on his retirement. Died 24 April 1934 at Kincairn, Blairs, Aberdeen. Medal was ordered after the Queen's death 13 February 1901, and was the last awarded. Refs.: *Who was Who.*

NOTE: Rankin, Gordon, Chidda and Michie do not appear in any printed register.

RECIPIENT OF THE SPECIAL SILVER MEDAL

Mr George Butcher

1896. Presented by Victoria R.I. to George Butcher Valet to HRH Prince Henry of Battenberg in recognition of his devoted and faithful services to his dear Master.

Valet to Prince Henry of Battenberg and later Steward to Princess Beatrice (Princess Henry of Battenberg). Received the Royal Victorian Medal (Silver) on 7 October 1904. Butcher also had the Ashanti Star 1896, Queen Victoria's Jubilee Medal (it is not known whether in silver or bronze or whether he received the 1887 medal with bar 1897 or the 1897 medal), Edward VII's Coronation Medal 1902 (Bronze) and George V's Coronation Medal 1911.

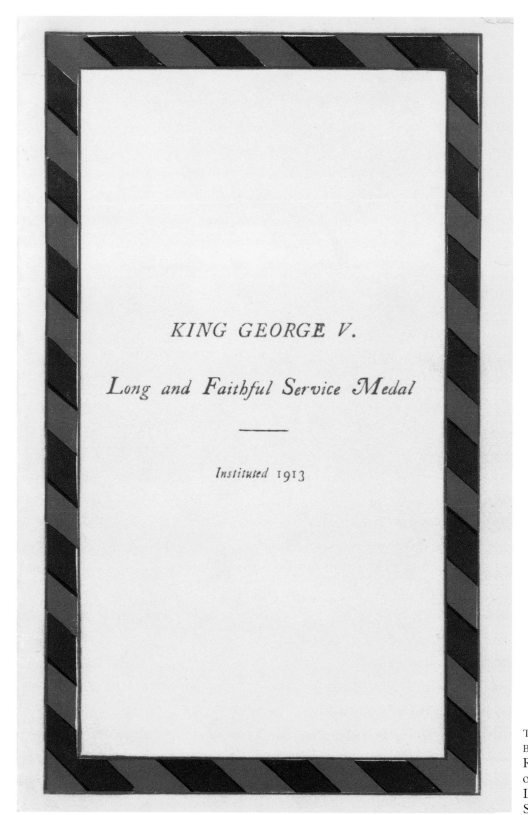

KING GEORGE V.

Long and Faithful Service Medal

———

Instituted 1913

THE COVER OF THE
BOOKLET of the
Rules and Regulations
of The King George V
Long and Faithful
Service Medal.

THE RULES AND REGULATIONS OF THE KING GEORGE V LONG AND FAITHFUL SERVICE MEDAL

———

GEORGE R.I.

GEORGE THE FIFTH by the Grace of God of the United Kingdom of Great Britain and Ireland, and of the British Dominions beyond the Seas, King, Defender of the Faith, Emperor of India, To all to whom these Presents shall come, Greeting: Whereas We have taken into Our Royal Consideration the long and faithful services to Our Person which are being and have been rendered by Our Servants both before, and after Our Succession to the Throne. And Whereas We are desirous of distinguishing such service by some mark of Our Royal Favour We do by these Presents for Us institute and create a Medal to be called and known by the name style and designation of "The Long and Faithful Service Medal" and We are hereby graciously pleased to make ordain and establish the following ordinances for the government of the same.

Firstly: It is ordained that the Long and Faithful Service Medal shall be a circular Medal of Silver surmounted by Our Royal Cypher ensigned with Our Imperial Crown having on the obverse Our Royal Effigy and on the reverse, an ornamental design with the words "For Long and Faithful Service" and shall bear on the rim the name of the person upon whom We are pleased to confer the said Decoration.

Secondly: It is ordained that the Medal shall be worn on the left breast of the coat or outer garment pendent to a riband of the breadth of one inch and a quarter consisting of red and blue diagonal stripes alternately of equal width immediately on the right of all other medals.

Thirdly: It is ordained that the Medal shall only be awarded to those Servants who shall have been in the service of Our Person for a period of at least twenty years, service to Us before Our succession to the Throne to be considered as forming part of the said period.

Fourthly: It is ordained that Servants of Our Household who shall have completed ten years additional service subsequent to receiving the said Medal shall, upon the recommendation of the Keeper of Our Privy Purse, have the said further service recorded by a Bar attached to the riband by which the said Medal is suspended and shall have every subsequent ten years service recorded by additional Bars subject nevertheless to Our Royal Sanction in each case.

Fifthly: It is ordained that the Keeper of Our Privy Purse for the time being shall be the custodian of this Our Royal Warrant and shall from time to time submit for Our consideration the names of such Servants as may be eligible to receive the said Medal and Bars, and further, shall keep a Register of the names of those upon whom We may be pleased to confer this Decoration.

Sixthly: It is ordained that upon the death of a recipient of the said Medal the latter shall remain in the possession of such recipient's representatives, no person however being entitled to wear the said Medal.

Seventhly: It is ordained that if any Servant upon whom We have been pleased to confer the Medal shall be guilty of such conduct as in Our judgement disqualifies such Servant from continuing to wear the same, the Medal shall be forfeited, and the name of the Servant shall be forthwith erased from the Register of those upon whom the said Decoration shall have been conferred.

Given at Our Court at Buckingham Palace the third day of June, 1913, in the fourth year of Our Reign

By His Majesty's Command,

William Carington,
Keeper of the Privy Purse.

Seventhly: It is ordained that if any Servant upon whom We have been pleased to confer the Medal shall be guilty of such conduct as in Our judgement disqualifies such Servant from continuing to wear the same, the Medal shall be forfeited, and the name of the Servant shall be forthwith erased from the Register of those upon whom the said Decorations shall have been conferred. And it is further ordained that every Servant upon whom the said Medal is conferred shall before receiving the Decoration, enter into an agreement to return the same if the name of such Servant shall be erased under this Ordinance.

Given at Our Court at Buckingham Palace the third day of June, 1913, in the fourth year of Our Reign

By His Majesty's Command,

William Carington,
Keeper of the Privy Purse.

PAGES FROM THE BOOKLET of the Rules and Regulations of The King George V Long and Faithful Service Medal.

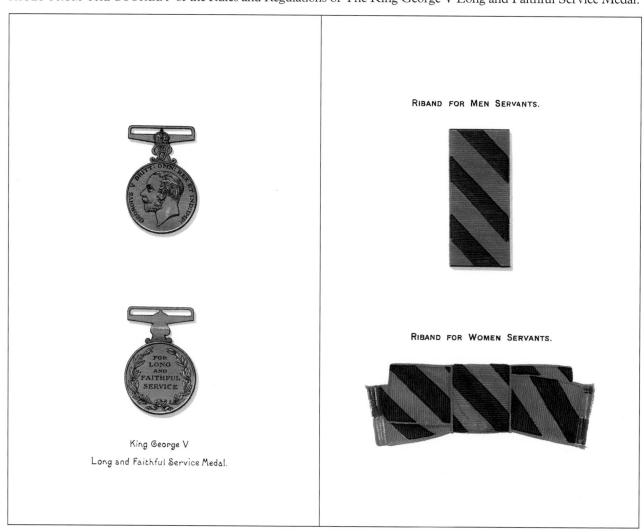

King George V
Long and Faithful Service Medal.

RIBAND FOR MEN SERVANTS.

RIBAND FOR WOMEN SERVANTS.

RECIPIENTS OF
THE KING GEORGE V
LONG AND FAITHFUL
SERVICE MEDAL

——

		30 years clasp	40 years clasp	50 years clasp
1913				
June	HOWLETT, Richard, *Principal Valet to HM*	1923	1933	
	WAKEFORD, Albert Edward, *Page of the Backstairs*	1923	1932	
	ALLAN, David, *Tapissier*	1923	1933	1943
	SHILLITO, Herbert, *Yeoman of the Silver Pantry*	1923	1933	
	POTTINGER, John, *Groom of the Cellars*	1923	1933	1 Feb 1943
	WOODS, Charles, *Assistant Usher of the Hall*	1923	1933	
	BALAAM, Ellen, *Head Housemaid*	1923		
	ROSE, Rizpah, *Housekeeper's Maid*	1923		
	STRATTON, George Henry, *Head Groom*	1923	1933	
	OSBORN, Joseph, *Coachman*	1925	1935	
September	SMISSEN, Edwin George, *Page of the Backstairs*	1923	1933	
1914				
March	TUBBS, William John, *Privy Purse Messenger*	1924	1934	
August	CLARK, Annie, *Housekeeper*	1924		
September	MACKAY, Jeannie, *Housekeeper*			
October	IVES, James, *Driver, Royal Mews*	1924		
1915				
July	BILL, Charlotte, *Nurse*			
October	WAGG, Herbert, *Livery Helper, Royal Mews*	1925		
1916				
July	FROST, Alfred, *Assistant, Silver Pantry*	1926		
1917				
June	GLENNY, Michael, *Lamplighter*			
February	SMITH, James Henry, *Commissionaire Messenger*			
November	COPPLE, James, *Page of the Presence*	1927	1 Nov 1937	
1918				
September	YOUNG, William F., *Valet to Prince Henry and Prince George*			
1919				
1920				
February	FIGG, William G., *Chauffeur*	1930		
1921				
November	JOHNSTON, Thomas, *Sergeant Footman*			
December	WHITWELL, Arthur, *Groom*	1932		

		30 years clasp	40 years clasp	50 years clasp

1922

		30 years clasp	40 years clasp	50 years clasp
January	BALAAM, Emily, *Linen Room Maid*			
	GARRATt, Henry Walter, *Livery Porter*	1932		
	JOWETT, Ernest, *Livery Porter*	1932	20 Jan 1942	
February	SAUNDERS, Harry, *Postillion*	1932		
March	TUCKEY, B.E., *Stable Foreman*			
	ALLAN, Alfred, *Joiner*	1932	7 Feb 1942	24 Feb 1952
	CLEMSON, James, *Stable Helper*			
	WELLER, George, *Stable Helper*			
April	THOMPSON, Frederick, *Outrider*			
May	CÉDARD, Henri, *Chef*	1932		
	NEWNHAM, Frederick, *Coachman*	1932		
July	WELLER, Henry, *Electrician*	1933		

1923

		30 years clasp	40 years clasp	50 years clasp
January	MILLER, Sidney John, *2nd Valet to HM*	1933		
February	COOK, Frederick, *Coal Porter*	1933		
	TAYLOR, Walter, *Under Butler*	1933		
	MARMOY, James, *Tapissier*			
April	BROWN, Ernest, *Footman*			
	PHILLIPS, Ernest, *Under Butler*			
	ANDREWS, H.F., *Postillion*			
November	GRANT, Jessie, *Kitchen Maid*	1933	11 Nov 1943	

1924

		30 years clasp	40 years clasp	50 years clasp
June	MOULD, F.J., *Coachman*	1935		
October	JARVIS, Annie, *Assistant Cook*	1934	1 Oct 1944	
	STOCKBRIDGE, Sarah, *Housemaid*	1935		
	PARNELL, Horace, *Stable Helper*	1934		

1925

		30 years clasp	40 years clasp	50 years clasp
February	FORSYTH, H.C., *Piper (later Extra Piper)*	1935	1 Feb 1945	
December	TINGLEY, George, *Driver*			

1926

		30 years clasp	40 years clasp	50 years clasp
January	CAPELL, E.P., *Chauffeur*	1936		
November	DOWNING, G., *Chauffeur*	17 Nov 1936		

1927

		30 years clasp	40 years clasp	50 years clasp
February	NEWTON, J.R., *Livery Porter*	7 Nov 1937	7 Nov 1947	
May	SHAW, Albert, *Coal Porter*			
	BECK, William, *Stable Helper*			
October	COX, Fanny E., *Housemaid*			

1928

		30 years clasp	40 years clasp	50 years clasp
January	WELLER, Emily, *Dresser to HM*	28 Jan 1938		
	AMOS, Alfred, *Gamekeeper*	3 Jan 1938	3 Jan 1948	
February	MERELL, D., *Stable Helper*			
	HUMFREY, Oscar, *Chauffeur*			
	SEABRIGHT, T., *Footman*			

1929

		30 years clasp	40 years clasp	50 years clasp
February	ARNOLD, Charles E., *Assistant, Steward's Room*			
	HARRIS, Percy, *Stable Helper*			
May	LAMBERT, Albert William, *Stable Helper*			
	POUPART, P.H., *Chef*			
	BUNNING, Mary, *Housekeeper, Frogmore*	6 May 1940		

	30 years clasp	40 years clasp	50 years clasp

1930

May

	30 years clasp	40 years clasp	50 years clasp
COLE, H., *State Page*			
HAMMETT, E., *Page of the Chambers*			
GOWER, J., *Page of the Backstairs*			
REYNOLDS, T., *Page of the Backstairs*			
THOMAS, A.W., *Page of the Backstairs*	6 May 1940	6 May 1950	
TWYMAN, A., *Page of the Backstairs*			
COLLINS, E., *Page of the Backstairs*			
HALL, B., *Page of the Presence 2nd Class*			
OSMOND, G., *Page of the Presence 2nd Class*	6 May 1940		
SNOWDON, T., *Page of the Presence 2nd Class*			
WOODBRIDGE, A., *Page of the Presence 2nd Class*			
HILL, S. P., *Pages' Man*			
WALKER, F., *Stewards Room, Pages' Man*			
TAYLOR, O.J., *Yeoman State Porter*			
MCLEOD, T., *Yeoman State Porter*			
RODDA, H.W., *Under State Porter*			
PUTTOCK, W., *Principal Gentleman Porter*			
POTTOW, J., *Yeoman Gentleman Porter*			
SCOTT, G., *Yeoman Gentleman Porter*			
KENNEDY, R., *Groom Gentleman Porter*			
ICKE, G., *Groom Gentleman Porter*			
DENCH, G., *Gentleman Porter*	6 May 1940		
DOWSETT, W., *Assistant Gentleman Porter*			
RAMSDALL, W., *Assistant Gentleman Porter*	6 May 1940		
BRANT, F., *Livery Porter*			
ELSON, J., *Livery Porter*			
HARRISON, H., *Livery Porter*			
HEEKS, A., *Livery Porter*			
NORTON, W., *Livery Porter*			
TAYLOR, C.E., *Livery Porter*			
VYSE, C.A., *Livery Porter*	1 Nov 1940		
WARREN, A., *Livery Porter*			
COX, F., *Porter, Windsor Castle*	6 May 1940		
ELMER, A., *Porter, Windsor Castle*	6 May 1940		
NEWBERRY, W., *Porter, Inspector's Staff, Buckingham Palace*			
FINCH, C., *Night Porter*			
GARDNER, J., *Night Porter*			
WELLS, W., *Night Porter*			
JEFFERIES, G., *Night Porter, Windsor Castle*			
FIRMIN, W., *Coal Porter*			
RIDGEON, A., *Coal Porter, Windsor Castle*			
ROGERS, J., *Assistant Coal Porter, Windsor Castle*			
GRAY, S.E., *Under Butler*			
GARRATT, E., *2nd Under Butler*	6 May 1940	6 May 1950	
KENNEDY, J., *Glass Under Butler*			
BAILEY, A.B., *Footman*	6 May 1940		
ELDER, A., *Footman*			
CRISP, W., *Brusher*			
NOON, Miss E., *Housekeeper, York Cottage*			
FRASER, Annie, *Head Housemaid, Holyrood*			
BAXTER, Clara, *Housemaid, Windsor Castle*			
CROSS, Ada, *Housemaid, Windsor Castle*			
GORDON, Annie, *Housemaid, Windsor Castle*	6 May 1940	6 May 1950	
KEELING, Effie, *Housemaid, Windsor Castle*			
WILLS, Frances, *Housemaid, Windsor Castle*			
WINN, Harriet, *Housemaid, Windsor Castle*			
DURRAN, Amelia, *Housemaid, Balmoral*			
CHISHOLM, Annie, *Linen Maid, Windsor Castle*			
CROSS, Sarah, *Linen Maid, Windsor Castle*			
FOOTE, Fanny, *Linen Maid, Windsor Castle*			
SYMONS, Eleanor, *Linen Room Maid*			
SIMMONS, Ellen, *Assistant Kitchen Maid*	6 May 1940		
LAWLESS, Catherine, *Basement Maid*			
REEVES, Minnie, *Basement Maid*			
DUNGER, Mrs Honor, *Kitchen Woman, Sandringham*	1940		
NURSE, Mrs Elizabeth, *Daily Woman, Sandringham*	1940		
GRACE, W., *Groom of Silver Pantry*			

	30 years clasp	40 years clasp	50 years clasp
WATTS, C., *2nd Yeoman of Silver Pantry*			
KEEP, G., *1st Assistant Silver Pantry*			
BRYANT, J., *Assistant Silver Pantry*	6 May 1940		
MOFFATT, E. G., *Groom of the Cellars*	15 Dec 1940	15 Dec 1950	
WEBLIN, F., *Groom of the Cellars*			
MCNAUGHTON, J.G., *Assistant in the Cellars*	17 Nov 1940		
SKENE, W., *1st Yeoman of the Wine Cellars*			
SHORTER, Frederick Edward, *2nd Yeoman of the Wine Cellars*			
MERCER, H., *1st Store Clerk*			
TWYNAM, A., *2nd Store Clerk*			
HARRISON, F., *Storekeeper, Windsor Castle*			
ELDER, J., *Messenger to Comptroller of Supply*			
TSCHUMI, G., *3rd Chef*			
WEATHERALL, H., *Roasting Cook*			
ETHERTON, W., *Steam Apparatus Man*			
FOWLER, W., *Lamplighter*			
WEEKLY, A., *Lamplighter*			
BAKER, F., *Coachman*			
GAINES, F., *Coachman*			
LINES, E., *Coachman*			
O'MARA, A., *Coachman*			
PRYOR, A., *Coachman*			
CLARKE, J.H., *Postillion*	6 May 1940		
CHAMPION, T., *Postillion*	6 May 1940		
FISHER, E.C., *Postillion*			
GIDDINS, G.E., *Postillion*			
LANGFORD, R., *Postillion*			
LAND, Rupert R., *Postillion*	6 May 1940	6 May 1950	
MURKING, W., *Postillion*	6 May 1940		
PRENTICE, G., *Postillion*			
PARR, Robert, *Postillion*	6 May 1940	6 May 1950	
SLACK, J., *Postillion*			
STANLEY, J., *Postillion*			
SIMMONDS, P., *Postillion*			
SHINER, G., *Postillion*			
WEST, S., *Postillion*			
BACON, W.J., *Groom*	6 May 1940	6 May 1950	
BEST, F.A., *Groom*	Apr 1943 (Broken time)		
DICKINSON, L.J.B., *Groom*	6 May 1940		
FRENCH, Charles, *Groom*			
GAME, T., *Groom*			
PUGH, E., *Groom*	6 May 1940		
BEAUMONT, W., *Outrider*			
BUNCE, A.J., *Driver*			
HOWARD, A., *Driver*			
NEWMAN, M., *Driver*			
TAYLOR, W.L., *Driver*	6 May 1940		
VENN, W., *Driver*	Apr 1943 (Broken time)		
HARDY, F., *Gate Porter*			
HAWKINS, F., *Gate Porter*	Apr 1943 (Broken time)		
MCILVEEN, F., *Gate Porter*	6 May 1940	6 May 1950	
BEAUMONT, A., *Gate Porter*			
SANDERS, F.J., *Stable Helper*			
FRANCIS, W., *Stud Helper*			
HALSE, J., *Stud Helper*			
PELLET, E.J., *Stud Helper*			
HODGES, Walter, *Stud, Hampton Court*	1940	1950	
GREEN, A., *Horsemaster*			
BROWN, W., *Shoeing Smith*			
MOORES, W., *Harness Cleaner*			
NORMAN, H., *Carriage Painter*			
COOPER, J.L., *Carriage Washer*			
DAY, W., *Carriage Washer*			
MINTER, A.F., *Carriage Washer*			
PRICE, E. J., *Carriage Washer*			
WRAIGHT, W., *Carriage Washer*	6 May 1940		
RAPLEY, J.E., *Storeman*			
CLARKE, E., *Canteen Man, Royal Mews*			

	30 years clasp	40 years clasp	50 years clasp
WAGG, Mrs Mary A., *Daily Help, Royal Mews, Buckingham Palace (Medal and Clasp awarded 1945)*	1940		
BARRY, F.W., *Royal Library, Windsor Castle*			
KEMP, E., *Inventory Clerk, Windsor Castle*			
VAUGHAN, F., *Binder, Royal Archives*			
SEYMOUR, A.G., *Inspector's Staff, Windsor Castle*			
ROBERTS, C., *Clerk, Inspector's Staff, Buckingham Palace*			
SEYMOUR, F., *Foreman, Inspector's Staff, Buckingham Palace*			
GROVE, C., *Caretaker, St James's Palace*			
ASH, S., *Office Keeper, Lord Chamberlain's Office*			
HYEM, P.W., *Office Keeper and Messenger*	1940	1950	
HAWKINS W., *King's Messenger*			
PEARCE, E., *Messenger, Lord Chamberlain's Office*	6 May 1940		
SMITH, W., *Messenger to Marshal of Diplomatic Corps*			
SMITH, F.H., *Privy Purse Messenger*			
BRADSHAW, G., *Leading Carpet Planner*			
WOORE, E., *Chief Carpet Planner, Windsor Castle*	Oct 1944 (Broken time)		
SPEARING, J., *Carpet Planner*			
GIBBINS, Sarah, *Carpet Sewer*			
CLEAVE, L., *Tapissier*			
JACKSON, C.J., *Chief Upholsterer*	6 May 1940		
WALLER, W., *Chief Upholsterer, Windsor Castle*			
COOPER, Ada, *Upholstress*			
JANAWAY, E., *Blindmaker, Windsor Castle*			
RAINBOW, E. J., *Chief Cabinet Maker (awarded 60-year clasp Apr 1970)*	6 May 1940	6 June 1950	2 Apr 1960
WILSON, G., *Chief Cabinet Maker*			
GILL, J.W.H., *French Polisher*			
JACKSON, E.C., *Ormolu Cleaner*	6 May 1940		
COPPERWHEAT, T., *Gilder*			
FELLOWS, A.H., *Metalsmith, Windsor Castle*			
MARVIN, H., *Stovesmith*			
WILKES, J., *Assistant Stovesmith*			
JENKINS, A., *Fluesman*	6 May 1940		
WOOD, E.A., *Electrician, Windsor Castle*			
FELLOWS, W. J., *Electrician, Windsor Castle*	6 May 1940		
FOLLAND, W. J., *Sergeant and Yeoman of the Vestry, Chapel Royal, St. James's Palace*			
BLAND, C., *Marshalman*	6 May 1940		
ELDER, A.L., *Marshalman*	6 May 1940		
PRICE, George, *Marshalman*	6 May 1940		
PARKER, W., *Marshalman*			
CAMPBELL, J., *Groom of the Great Chamber*			
PERRINS, T., *Attendant in State Apartments*			
SEYMOUR, E.J., *Attendant in State Apartments*			
BROWN, H., *State Room Porter*			
FITCH, E. *State Room Fireman*	6 May 1940	6 May 1950	
BRINDLEY, E., *State Room Fireman*			
ABERCROMBIE, J., *Head Stalker*			
GORDON, F., *Stalker*	6 May 1940		
TORRY, J., *Stalker*			
BRUCE, James, *Balmoral**	1940		
COLLIE, Wolseley, *Balmoral**	1940		
MCGREGOR, James, *Balmoral**	1940	6 May 1950	
ROBERTSON, William, *Balmoral**	1940	6 May 1950	
STEWART, Francis, *Balmoral**	1940		
BROWN, Leopold, *Windsor Royal Gardens**	1940	1950	
GREEN, William, *Windsor Royal Gardens**	1940		
GODLIMAN, Jacob, *Windsor Royal Gardens**	1940	1950	
HAILE, Norman, *Windsor Royal Gardens**	1940		
HOPCROFT, Thomas, *Windsor Royal Gardens**	1940		
HUGHES, Alfred, *Windsor Royal Gardens**	1940		
LANFEAR, James, *Windsor Royal Gardens**	1940		
MOORE, Walter, *Windsor Royal Gardens**	1940	1950	
MAY, Arthur J., *Windsor Royal Gardens**	1940	1950	
MERRYMAN, Edward, *Windsor Royal Gardens**	1940	1950	
NEIGHBOUR, Albert, *Windsor Royal Gardens**	1940		
NEIL, Herbert J., *Windsor Royal Gardens**	1940		
RALPH, Alfred, *Windsor Royal Gardens**	1940	1950	

	30 years clasp	40 years clasp	50 years clasp
SIMMONDS, John, *Windsor Royal Gardens*★	1940		
WEATHERALL, Richard, *Windsor Royal Gardens*★	1940		
WILSON, Charles, *Windsor Royal Gardens*★	1940		
BAILEY, John, *Windsor Royal Gardens*★	1940		
BROWN, Frederick G., *Windsor Royal Gardens*★	1940	1950	
BLAND, F.W., *Head Keeper, Sandringham*			
BRIDGES, F.J., *Keeper, Sandringham*			
BRIDGES, F.T.J., *Keeper, Sandringham*	Feb 1940		
BRIDGES, R., *Keeper, Sandringham*	6 May 1940		
GAMBLE, T., *Keeper, Sandringham*			
GOODSHIP, W., *Keeper, Sandringham*			
PLEVIN, H., *Keeper, Sandringham*			
WALKER, T., *Keeper, Sandringham*	6 May 1940		
WATTS, A., *Keeper, Sandringham*			
WILLIAMS, R.K., *Keeper, Sandringham*	6 May 1940		
COX, Percy A., *Sandringham Stud*★	1940	1950	
ALLEN, Ernest E., *Sandringham*★	1940		
ANNISON, Joseph, *Sandringham*★	1940		
BATTERBEE, George, *Sandringham*★	1940	1950	
BOUGHEN, E., *Sandringham*★	1940		
BANSTEAD, William H., *Sandringham*★	1940		
BOND, John, *Sandringham*★	1940	1950	
BUGG, Henry F., *Sandringham*★	1940		
BIRD, Jack, *Sandringham*★	1940		
BUNN, Frederick C., *Sandringham*★	1940	1950	
BRIDGES, Wilfred G., *Sandringham*★	1940	1950	
BURROUGH, Samuel H., *Sandringham*★	1940		
COLLISON, Frederick, *Sandringham*★	1940		
COLEMAN, Charles H., *Sandringham*★	1940	1950	
CROWE, Robert J., *Sandringham*★	1940	1950	
COE, Arthur R., *Sandringham*★	1940		
DUNGER, Robert J., *Sandringham*★	1940		
DUNGER, Albert, *Sandringham*★	1940	1950	
DAW, Robert J., *Sandringham*★	1940		
DAW, Frederick, *Sandringham*★	1940	1950	
DAW, Sidney W., *Sandringham*★	1940	1950	
DAW, William J., *Sandringham*★	1940	1950	
DYE, Edward, *Sandringham*★	1940		
DANIELS, Sydney, *Sandringham*★	1940		
DUNCAN, William W., *Sandringham*★	1940	1950	
EMMERSON, James E., *Sandringham*★	1940	1950	
GREEN, James E., *Sandringham*★	1940		
GENT, John William, *Sandringham*★	1940	1950	
GODFREY, William J., *Sandringham*★	1940		
GIBSON, Robert, *Sandringham*★			
GOODSHIP, Sydney W., *Sandringham*★	1940	1950	
GRIMES, James, *Sandringham*★	1940		
HOWELL, David G., *Sandringham*★	1940	1950	
HARDY, Herbert, *Sandringham*★	1940		
HOUCHEN, George J., *Sandringham*★	1940		
HOUCHEN, Thomas, *Sandringham*★	1940	1950	
HARLOW, Frank, *Sandringham*★	1940		
HAMMOND, Robert J., *Sandringham*★	1940	1950	
LINES, Sydney A., *Sandringham*★	1940	ret. 1949	
LINES, Albert E., *Sandringham*★	1940	1950	
LEE, Arthur E., *Sandringham*★	1940	1950	
MERRIKIN, Herbert, *Sandringham*★	1940	1950	
SOANES, James W., *Sandringham*★	1940	1950	
SENTER, John, *Sandringham*★	1940		
TURLEY, Frederick P., *Sandringham*★	1940	1950	
THREADKILL, Percy W., *Sandringham*★	1940	1950	
WATERS, Arthur, *Sandringham*★	1940		

1931

	30 years clasp	40 years clasp	50 years clasp
LUCAS, E.J., *Page of the Presence*	15 Mar 1941	15 Mar 1951	
NICOLSON, J.F., *Sergeant Footman*			
HIGGINS, H.G., *Porter, Windsor Castle*	5 Nov 1940		
WATERS, F., *Assistant, Silver Pantry*	30 Jan 1940		

	30 years clasp	40 years clasp	50 years clasp
BOSHER, T., *2nd Roasting Cook*			
WEATHERLY, J.E., *Usher, Servants Hall*	10 Apr 1941	10 Apr 1951	
MUNDAY, Alice, *Housemaid*	18 Apr 1941		
WILLIAMS, Isabella, *Housemaid, Windsor Castle*			
BUTCHER, Sarah M., *Housekeeper, Sandringham*	18 Apr 1941	Feb 1951	
HICKMAN, Rosella R., *Head Linen Maid, Sandringham*	28 Aug 1941	Aug 1951	
CROSS, Mrs Elizabeth, *Daily Help, Sandringham*	1941		
(*Medal and Clasp awarded 1945*)			
LINES, Miss Sarah, *Daily Help*	1941	1951	
BURTON, C.G., *Caretaker, Royal Pavilion, Aldershot*			
HOUSE, F.B., *Inventory Clerk*			
ATACK, H.J., *Polisher*	7 Mar 1941		
COTTERAL, G.W., *Outrider*	22 Oct 1940	22 Oct 1950	
SAWYER, E.J., *Stable Helper*	26 Aug 1940		
WILES, R., *Stable Helper*	8 Jan 1941		
ABSOLOM, F. H., *Stable Helper*	11 Sept 1940	11 Sept 1950	
WAY, G.R., *Liveried Gamekeeper, Sandringham*	Apr 1941		
MITCHELL, Arthur E., *Sandringham* ★	1941		
NURSE, Ernest, *Sandringham* ★	1941	1951	
RICHES, Geo. W., *Sandringham* ★	1941	1951	1961
SEAMAN, James, *Sandringham* ★	1941		

1932

	30 years clasp	40 years clasp	50 years clasp
MASON, F., *Steward, HM Yacht* Britannia	11 Mar 1942	11 Mar 1952	
BLYFIELD, A., *Livery Porter*	1 Dec 1941		
COMBER, E., *Under Butler*	1 Nov 1941	1 Nov 1951	
BENSTEAD, R., *Assistant in Silver Pantry*	1942	1952	
STOKES, John H., *Assistant, Steward's Room*	18 Nov 1941	18 Nov 1951	
COMMON, J., *House Porter, Holyroodhouse*	7 Oct 1941		
RAYMENT, H., *Drawing Room Porter, Windsor Castle*			
RAWLINGS, Amelia, *Housekeeper, Windsor Castle*			
MCKIE, Elizabeth, *Resident Housemaid, Holyroodhouse*			
LOMATH, Mildred, *Head Coffee Room Maid*			
GLEN, Emily, *Housemaid*	1 Apr 1942	1 Apr 1952	
INSLEY, Oswaldina, *Housemaid*	Mar 1946	Oct 1952 (Broken time)	
QUANTRILL, F.A., *Privy Purse Messenger*	8 Aug 1941	8 Aug 1951	
PARSONS, F.E., *Royal Library, Windsor Castle*			
COMBER, J., *Gilder, Windsor Castle*	9 May 1941	9 May 1951	
DUNN, R., *Marshalman*	16 Nov 1941	16 Nov 1951	
WHINCUP, J., *Postillion*			
TRIBBLE, W., *Stable Helper*	Feb 1942		
FRENCH, C., *Liveried Gamekeeper, Sandringham*	Apr 1942		
LAMONT, Charles, *Balmoral* ★	1942	May 1952	
LINES, Walter L., *Sandringham* ★			
ANNESS, F.J., *Store Clerk*			

1933

	30 years clasp	40 years clasp	50 years clasp
LINNETT, George, *Master of Household's Department*	1943		
(*formerly Royal Gardens*)			
INCHBOLD, P., *Porter, Windsor Castle*			
POTTINGER, G., *1st Kitchen Porter*	7 July 1942		
RENN, H., *Coal Porter, Windsor Castle*			
SYMONDS, Anne, *Housekeeper, Hampton Court*	1 Jan 1941	1 Jan 1951	
DEWAR, Marjory, *Housemaid*	14 Feb 1943	14 Feb 1953	
MORRIS, Kate, *Housemaid, Windsor Castle*			
KELLY, Mrs Alice Maud Mary, *Temporary Washer-up,*	1943	1953	
Buckingham Palace (*Medal and Clasp given 10 Oct 1945*)			
EDMONSTONE, J.R., *Foreman, Holyrood*	15 Nov 1942	15 Nov 1952	
TESTER, W., *Assistant Upholsterer, Windsor Castle*			
TAYLOR, Kate, *Head Needlewoman, Windsor Castle*	30 Dec 1942		
HILL, G.E., *Postillion*	31 Aug 1942		
CROFT, H., *Stable Helper*	13 Oct 1942		
LAKE, W.F., *Stable Helper*	4 Aug 1942		
WYLDE, F.T., *Messenger, Royal Mews*	1 Dec 1942	1 Dec 1952	
BARNARD, W., *Marshalman*			
KIMBER, C., *Royal Pavilion, Aldershot*			

	30 years clasp	40 years clasp	50 years clasp
MACKINTOSH, Victor A.C., *Balmoral*	1943	1953	
BROWN, Charles H., *Windsor, Royal Gardens*★	1943	7 Sept 1952	
CANNON, John, *Windsor, Royal Gardens*	1943		
BRIDGER, Frederick Walter, *Farm Helper, Hampton Court*	1943	20 May 1952	
BATTERBEE, Robert J., *Sandringham*★	1943		
NURSE, James, *Sandringham*★	1943	1953	
WELLS, Albert R., *Sandringham*★	1943	1953	1963

1934

DEAL, W.G., *Under Butler*	20 Aug 1943		
SPELLER, Mary, *Housemaid*	15 July 1944		
BOYCE, A.G., *Office Porter, Inspector's Staff, Windsor Castle*	June 1944		
FELLOWS, Gertrude Edith, *Needlewoman, Inspector's Staff, Windsor Castle*	1 Dec 1943	1 Dec 1953	
WRIGHT, Jessie, *Upholsteress*			
PACE, A.E., *Stable Helper*	27 July 1943		
HOOKS, S.E., *Liveried Gamekeeper, Sandringham*	Nov 1943	12 Nov 1953	1 Nov 1963
BRIDGES, Albert G., *Sandringham*★	1944		
COLLINSON, George, *Sandringham*★	1944		
GRIMES, Robert, *Sandringham*★	1 Sept 1944		
RANSOME, Frank L., *Sandringham*★	1944		
YALLOP, George W., *Sandringham*★	1944		
BATES, R.E., *Sandringham*	1944	1955	

1935

BRADLEY, H., *Livery Porter*			
BARRANCE, R., *Livery Porter*	22 Feb 1945		
PUGH, Margaret, *Housemaid, Buckingham Palace*			
DAY, Mary, *Extra Assistant in Silver Pantry*			
FRASER, J., *Staff of the Palace at Holyroodhouse*	4 Aug 1944	4 Aug 1954	
JONES, J.E., *Groom, Royal Mews*	4 Sept 1944		
PANTER, J., *Stable Helper, Buckingham Palace*			
BUSS, E., *Yard Man, Royal Mews*			
EARWAKER, F.G., *Gate Porter, Royal Mews*			
CATT, B.C., *Shoeing Smith*			
METCALFE, M., *Canteen Man, Royal Mews*			
FARRELLY, P., *Nightwatchman, Royal Mews*	27 Sept 1944		
BLACK, P., *Marshalman*			
MORRISON, John William, *Balmoral*	18 May 1945	18 May 1955	
SEARS, John R., *Windsor Royal Gardens*★	1 Jan 1945		
PARKER, William Henry, *Windsor Royal Gardens*★	25 May 1945		
WELLING, A. William, *Windsor Royal Gardens*★	1 Jan 1945		
SOUTHWELL, Percy F., *Sandringham*★	Mar 1945	1 Mar 1955	
SOUTHGATE, James, *Sandringham*★	1 Jan 1945		
ASKER, Edward J., *Sandringham*★	May 1945		
BROWN, William, *Sandringham*★	May 1945		
BATTERBEE, Daniel E.G., *Sandringham*★	1945		
BROWN, Ernest E., *Sandringham Stud*★	May 45	1 Mar 1955	1 Mar 1965
CRADDOCK, J., *Yeoman of Signals, Windsor Castle*	1913–1936		
COPSEY, G., *Porter Inspector's Staff, Windsor Castle*			
KEATING, Mrs M., *Housekeeper*	1 Jan 1946	1 Jan 1956	
BARNES, E.G., *Messenger, Central Chancery of the Orders of Knighthood*			
ATHOW, Thomas, *Sandringham*★	Sept 1946		
BOUGHEN, Leslie V., *Sandringham*★	1946		
GRIMES, Arthur, *Sandringham*★	Oct 1946	1 Jan 1956	
WOODHOUSE, Horace, *Sandringham*★	Mar 1946		

RECIPIENTS OF
THE KING GEORGE V HOUSEHOLD
LONG SERVICE TOKENS

═══

1930

Balmoral
Beddie E.G.
Bruce, J.†
Chalmers, R.T.
Collie, G.
Collie, W.†
Duguid, C.
Duguid, J.
Duncan, P.
Durran, W.
Durran, J.
Edmonston, J.
Howie, G.
McDonald, A.
McGregor, J.†
McGregor, J.
Morrison, W.
McDougall, W.
  (Senior)
Nicholson, J.
Robertson, W.†
Rose, D.
Stewart, D.
Stewart, F.†
Smith, Mary

Sandringham
Allen, E.E.†
Annison, J.†
Boughen, G.W.
Batterbee, G.†
Boughen, E.J.†
Benstead, W.H.
Bond, J.†
Bridges, A.
Bugg, H.†
Brown, J.
Bird, J.†
Benstead, R.
Bunn, F.C.†
Bridges, W.†
Buckett, W.
Burrough, S.H.†
Collinson, F.†
Crowe, R.
Crowe, R.J.†
Crowe, F.H.
Coe, A.R.†
Crisp, J.
Cox, P.†
Cook, C.
Cook, T.H.
Cross H.
Dunger, R.J.†
Dyble, M.
Daw, R.J.†
Dunger, A.†
Dye, G.W.
Drew, T.
Daw, F.†
Deaves, G.
Dolman, J.

Daniels, E.
Daw, S.W.†
Dye, E.†
Daniels, S.†
Duncan W.†
Daw, W.J.†
Emmerson, J.E.†
Flegg, R.H.
Finch, J.S.
Grief, J.H.
Grimes, J.
Green, J.E.†
Gent, J.W.†
Godfrey, W.J.†
Gent, A.W.
Gibson, R.†
Grimes, J.E.A.†
Goodship, S.†
Howell, D.†
Hurn, F.
Hardy, H.†
Houchen, T.†
Houchen, G.†
Hodges, C.
Hodges, W.†
Harlow, F.†
Hammond, R.†
Hooks, G.†
Harrod, G.W.
Haverley, T.G.
Johnson, H.
Jex, H.E.
Jakeman, W.H.
Lines, A.E.†
Lines, S.A.†
Lines, J.W.
Lee, A.†
Melton, G.N.
Melton, F.W.
Melton, F.
Melton, A.G.
Morgan, F.
Marrington, D.C.
Melton, E.H.
Merrikin, H.E.†
Painter, W.
Pattingale, V.A.E.
Riches, A.J.
Riches, John
Riches, James
Robbins, H.
Riches, H.
Rush, J.
Robinson, W.
Richardson, R.
Shread, H.
Simmons, J.
Soanes, J.W.†
Smith, P.J.
Steel, W.
Threadkill, P.W.†
Turley, F.P.†

Upstone, D.
Waters, A.†
Wells, G.E.
Wells, F.
Walton, R.G.
Walker, E.
Wade, A.J.
Yallop, E.
Simmons, A.
Smith, F.W.
Senter, J.†
Sayer, J.A.
Smith, F.

Gamekeeper Windsor Park
Fryett, F.
Bitmead, J.
Brown, L.†
Cox, V.
Emmerson, W.
Fuller, F.
Green, W.†
Godliman, J.†
Haile, N.†
Harmsworth, H.
Hoare, J.
Hopcroft, T.†
Hughes, A.†
Hubbard, A.
Hicks, W.
Hobday, R.
Langfear, J.†
Moore, W.†
May, A.†
Merryman, E.†
Neighbour, A.†
Palmer, J.
Phillips, J.
Ralph, A.†
Simmonds, J.†

Windsor Royal Gardens
Simmons, H.
Tilby, J.
Wilson, C.†
Weatherall, R.†

Windsor Royal Farms
Bartlett, R.
Laley, W.
Neil, Herbert†
Bailey, J.†
Brown, F.†

1931

Sandringham
Daniels, G.R.
Mitchell A.E.†
Nurse, E.
Riches, G.W.†
Seaman, J.†

Windsor Royal Farms
Higgs, H.
Wheeler, T.

† Long Service Token exchanged for Medal.

1932

Balmoral   Lamont, C.†
Sandringham   Bridges, M.
                  Daniels, W.A.
                  Lines, W.L.†

1933

Balmoral   Mackintosh, V.†

1933

Sandringham   Asker, W.†
                       Batterbee, R.J.†
                       Nurse, J.†
                       Riches, W.J.
                       Wells, A.R.†
Windsor Royal   Brown, C.†
Gardens   Cannon, J.†
                       Linnett, G.†
                       Newell, R.
                       Waltham, C.

1934

Sandringham   Asker, C.W.
                  Bridges, A.G.†
                  Bates, R.E.
                  Collinson, G.†
                  Chilleystone, J.H.
                  Grimes, R.†
                  Yallop, G.W.†
                  Ransome, F.†
                  Riches, P.E.

1935

Balmoral   Morrison, John W.†
Sandringham   Asker, E.†
                       Brown, W.†
                       Batterbee, D.†
                       Harper, A.
                       Hipkin, W.
                       Southwell, P.†
                       Watts, H.

Sandringham   Brown, E.†
Stud   Southgate, A.†
Windsor Royal   Parker, W.†
Gardens   Seares, J.†
                       Welling, W.†

1936

Sandringham   Athow, T.†
                  Boughen, L.†
                  Grimes, A.†
                  Hurn, J.F.
                  Hurst, A.
                  Stewart, J.
                  Woodhouse, H.J.†

† Long Service Token exchanged for Medal.

THE RULES AND REGULATIONS OF KING GEORGE VI LONG AND FAITHFUL SERVICE MEDAL

——

GEORGE R.I.

GEORGE THE SIXTH, by the Grace of God, of Great Britain, Ireland, and the British Dominions beyond the Seas, King, Defender of the Faith, Emperor of India, to all to whom these Presents shall come,

GREETING!

WHEREAS We have taken into Our Royal Consideration the long and faithful services to Our Person which are being and have been rendered by Our Servants both before, and after Our Accession to the Throne.

And whereas We are desirous of distinguishing such service by some mark of Our Royal Favour We do by these Presents for Us institute and create a Medal to be called and known by the name style and designation of the "Long and Faithful Service Medal" and We are hereby graciously pleased to make ordain and establish the following ordinances for the government of the same.

Firstly: It is ordained that the Long and Faithful Service Medal shall be a circular Medal of Silver surmounted by Our Royal Cypher ensigned with Our Imperial Crown having on the obverse Our Royal Effigy and on the reverse, an ornamental design with the words "For Long and Faithful Service" and shall bear on the rim the name of the person upon whom We are pleased to confer the said Medal.

Secondly: It is ordained that the Medal shall be worn on the left breast of the coat or outer garment pendent to a riband of the width of one inch consisting of red and blue diagonal stripes alternatively of equal width sloping towards the right arm, that it shall be worn immediately after King George the Fifth's Long and Faithful Service Medal, and that the last named Medal shall be worn, in future, immediately after Jubilee, Coronation and Durbar Medals.

Provided that when the Medal is worn by a woman, it may be worn on the left shoulder, suspended from a riband of the same width and colour, fashioned into a bow.

Thirdly: It is ordained that the Medal shall only be awarded to those Servants who shall have been for a period of at least twenty years in the service of Our Person, service to Us before Our Accession to the Throne being considered as forming part of the said period, or in the service of Her Majesty the Queen since Her Majesty's Marriage to Us or after Our Accession, or in the service of Our Royal Father, His late Majesty King George the Fifth, after His Accession to the Throne, or in the service of Our Royal Brother King Edward the Eighth after His creation as Prince of Wales or after his Accession to the Throne and up to the time of Our Accession, or in the service of Our Royal Mother, Queen Mary, either during the Reign of Our Royal Father or subsequently, service in any of the aforesaid capacities being aggregated.

Provided that holders of the "Long and Faithful Service Medal" instituted by Our Royal Father, His late Majesty King George the Fifth, shall not be eligible for the Medal instituted by this Our Warrant until they have been at least twenty years in the service of Our Person, service to Us before Our Accession to the Throne being considered as forming part of the said period, or in the Service of Her Majesty Queen Mary, subsequent to the date of Our Accession, service in the aforesaid capacities being aggregated.

Fourthly: It is ordained that Servants of Our Household or of Her Majesty the Queen's Household or of the Household of Her Majesty Queen Mary who, subsequent to receiving the said Medal instituted by this Our Warrant, shall have completed ten years additional service as defined in the first part of the Third Clause of this Warrant, shall, upon the recommendation of the Keeper of Our Privy Purse, be awarded a Clasp in respect of the said further service, the Clasp to be attached to the riband by which the said Medal is suspended, and shall in respect of every subsequent ten years of service be awarded additional Clasps subject nevertheless to Our Royal Sanction in each case.

Fifthly: It is ordained that those Servants of Our Household, or of Her Majesty the Queen's Household, or of the Household of Her Majesty Queen Mary who have been awarded the Long and Faithful Service Medal instituted by Our Royal Father, His late Majesty King George the Fifth shall in respect of each further ten years additional service as defined in the first part of the Third Clause of this Our Warrant be eligible for the award of a Clasp to the aforesaid Medal instituted by His late Majesty. The award of a Clasp or Clasps accordingly in respect, partly or wholly, of any service which would be reckoned towards the period of twenty years mentioned in the proviso to the Third Clause of this Our Warrant shall not prevent the reckoning of such service under that proviso.

Sixthly: It is ordained that the Keeper of Our Privy Purse for the time being shall be the custodian of this Our Royal Warrant and shall from time to time submit for Our consideration the names of such Servants as may be eligible to receive the said Medal and Clasps, and further, shall keep a Register of the names of those upon whom We may be pleased to confer this Medal.

Seventhly: It is ordained that upon the death of a recipient of the said Medal the latter shall remain in the possession of such recipient's representatives, no person however being entitled to wear the said Medal.

Eighthly: It is ordained that reproductions of the Long and Faithful Service Medal, known as a Miniature Medal, which may be worn on certain occasions by those to whom the Medal is awarded, shall be half the size of the Long and Faithful Service Medal.

Ninthly: It is ordained that if any Servant upon whom We have been pleased to confer the Medal shall be guilty of such conduct as in the judgement of Us, Our Heirs and Successors, disqualifies such Servant from continuing to wear the same, the Medal shall be forfeited, and the name of the Servant shall be forthwith erased from the Register of those upon whom the said Medal shall have been conferred: provided that it shall be competent for Us, Our Heirs and Successors to restore the Medal so forfeited.

Given at Our Court at St. James's, the twelfth day of November, 1943, in the seventh year of Our Reign.

By His Majesty's Command,

Ulick Alexander,
Keeper of the Privy Purse.

RECIPIENTS OF
THE KING GEORGE VI
LONG AND FAITHFUL
SERVICE MEDAL

═══

	30 years clasp	40 years clasp	50 years clasp
1936			
February RINGER, Thomas H., *Sandringham Farm*	Feb 1946		
March BROWN, Frederick John, *Sandringham*	Mar 1946	Mar 1956	
May MORGAN, Edward J.F., *Sandringham, Carpenters Yard*	May 1946	May 1956	
October BARLOW, John William, *Sandringham Woods*			
December DICKSON, John, *Foreman, Kitchen Garden, Windsor*	16 Dec 1946		
MOORE, James Frederick, *Labourer, Kitchen Garden, Windsor*	Dec 1946		
1937			
February PASCOE, Sidney Alfred, *Foreman, Fruit Houses Windsor Royal Gardens*	9 Feb 1947		
March NURSE, Herbert, *Sandringham Woods*	16 Mar 1947		
MATTHEWS, George William, *Labourer, Kitchen Gardens, Windsor*			
May BRIDGES, Thomas, *Sandringham, Carpenters Yard*			
GOOSEMAN, Constance, *Housemaid, Buckingham Palace*			
STEEL, Horace Jack, *Sandringham, Carpenters Yard*	14 May 1947	14 May 1957	14 May 1967
September TWITE, Wallace Jack, *Sandringham Woods*	15 Sept 1947	1 Sept 1957	1 Sept 1967
October GOLL, Frederick, *Sandringham Farm*			
November CRISP, Horace, *Sandringham, Carpenters Yard* (*Died in service very near to completing 50 years, Bar awarded to his widow January 1968*)	5 Nov 1947	5 Nov 1957	
December JEFFERY, Murray, *Carnation Grower, Royal Gardens, Windsor*	17 Dec 1937	17 Dec 1947	
1938			
February THOMPSON, Cecil Robert, *Chauffeur, Queen Mary's Household*	17 Feb 1948		
GOODSHIP, Reginald V., *Sandringham, Carpenters Yard*	Feb 1948		
May HOOKS, Alec L., *Sandringham Woods*	May 1948		
June HOOKS, Robert J.H., *Sandringham Gardener*	June 1948	June 1958	
July BARRY, Sydney G., *Assistant, Windsor Royal Library*	1 July 1948		
MCGREGOR, William, *Gardener, then Gatekeeper, Balmoral*	1 July 1948	1 July 1958	1 July 1968
August MILES, Arthur Thomas, *Labourer, Windsor Royal Gardens*	10 Aug 1948		
EASTWICK, Sydney J., *Game Department, Sandringham*	Aug 1948		
LINES, Stanley, *Woods, Sandringham*	Aug 1948	Aug 1958	18 Aug 1968
September RICHES, Arthur Robert, *Shepherd, Sandringham*	Sept 1948	Sept 1958	
October SOUTHGATE, Albert E., *Gardener, Sandringham*			
November BLAND, Edward, *Messenger, Buckingham Palace*			
December SAYER, George H., *Engineer, Sandringham* (*Joined 8 Nov 1918, not 3 Dec*)	3 Dec 1948	3 Dec 1958	8 Nov 1968
FRASER, Thomas, *Balmoral, Golf Course*	9 Dec 1948		
DICKINSON, Annie, *Housemaid, Buckingham Palace* (*Left 31 July 1939. Medal sent to her 9 June 1947*)			
1939			
January BURGESS, Frederick C., *Postillion, Royal Mews*	6 Jan 1949		
February CUNNINGHAM, Alexander Y., *Porter, Palace of Holyroodhouse*	5 Feb 1949	5 Feb 1959	
EMMERSON, Arthur R., *Sandringham, Carpenters Yard*	5 Feb 1949		

		30 years clasp	40 years clasp	50 years clasp
	WASEY, Eric, *Sandringham, Carpenters Yard*	7 Feb 1949		
	WOOLWAY, James, *Postillion and Driver, Royal Mews*	11 Feb 1949		
	DORRINGTON, George, *Carpet Planner, Superintendent's Staff, Buckingham Palace*			
	GRAY, Owen J., *Assistant Gentleman Porter*	15 Feb 1949		
	KEMP, John H., *Page of the Backstairs*	20 Feb 1949	20 Feb 1959	
March	ALLEN, John William, *Sandringham Woods*	Mar 1949	15 Mar 1959	
April	MITCHELL, Frederick C., *2nd Yeoman of the Royal Cellars*	1 Apr 1949		
	BOSHER, Alfred, *Kitchen Porter*			
June	CRISP, Horace J., *Page of the Presence*	10 June 1949		
	BATEMAN, William J., *Inventory Clerk, Superintendent's Staff, Windsor Castle*	21 June 1949	21 June 1959	
	BUNCE, Henry, *Carpet Planner, Superintendent's Staff, Windsor Castle*	28 June 1949		
	THOMAS, Evan, *Storesmith, Superintendent's Staff, Windsor Castle*			
August	MCLAUGHLIN, James, *Lorry Driver, Royal Gardens Windsor*	1 Aug 1949		
	STEPHEN, William, *Joiner, Balmoral*			
	GORE, David, *Sandringham, Woods*	9 Aug 1949		
October	WELLS, Horace, *Attendant, State Appartments, Windsor Castle*			
	MACDONALD, William, *Balmoral, Forestry*	17 Oct 1949		
	EDGECUMBE, Walter, *Livery Porter*			
	REED, Frederick J., *Yeoman, Royal Cellars*	27 Oct 1949		
	AYLMER, Albert Edward, *Sandringham, Farm*			
December	LARRINGTON, Walter F., *Sandringham, Farm*	12 Dec 1949	12 Dec 1959	
	BISSETT, Robert, *Balmoral, Forestry*	13 Dec 1949	13 Dec 1959	

1940

		30 years clasp	40 years clasp	50 years clasp
January	URQUHART, William, *Balmoral, Forestry*	26 Jan 1949		
	GAMBLE, Eric, *Carpenter's Yard, Sandringham*	Jan 1950	1 Jan 1960	
February	ANDOW, Arthur E., *Yardman, Royal Mews*	1 Feb 1950		
	BORLEY, Benjamin, *Carpenter's Yard, Sandringham*	Feb 1950		
	HUMPHREY, Arthur, *Carpenter's Yard, Sandringham*	Feb 1950		
March	ALLENBY, Richard, *Gilder, Superintendent's. Staff, Buckingham Palace*	6 Mar 1950		
	KENNEDY, George, *Sergeant Farrier, Royal Mews*			
	MANN, Ernest, *Blacksmith, Sandringham*			
April	SHEPHERD, Edward, *Head Messenger, Privy Purse*	14 Apr 1950		
	MCPHERSON, Alexander G., *Balmoral*	19 Apr 1950		
May	CLARK, Arthur, *State Room Porter*			
July	WEBSTER, James, *Gardener, Balmoral*	3 July 1950		
August	MARS, Ernest John, *Coal and Night Porter, Palace of Holyroodhouse*	7 Aug 1950		
	CHURCHER, Albert J., *Messenger, Privy Purse*			
September	AYLMER, Charles, *Sandringham, Woods*			
October	BOND, Horace L.L., *Carpenter's Yard, Sandringham*	8 Oct 1950	8 Oct 1960	8 Oct 1970
November	BURGESS, Henry, *Chauffeur, Royal Mews*			
	ROBERTSON, Jessie, *Head Housemaid, Sandringham*	1 Nov 1950	1 Nov 1960	

1941

		30 years clasp	40 years clasp	50 years clasp
January	HANSLIP, Walter J., *Carving School Sandringham*	3 Jan 1951		
February	RICHES, Albert Harry, *Kitchen Porter*	1 Feb 1951		
May	INKSTER, David White, *Electrician, Balmoral*	3 May 1951		
	LEE, George Green, *Carpenter's Yard, Sandringham*	11 May 1951		
August	ABERCROMBIE, James Jnr, *Stalker, Balmoral*			
	CRISP, Robert P., *Cabinet Maker, Windsor Castle*	7 Aug 1951	7 Aug 1961	
	CLARK, John Cummings, *Head Herdsman, Royal Farms*	10 Aug 1951		
September	BOUGHEN, Donald E.W., *Carpenter's Yard, Sandringham*	2 Sept 1951	2 Sept 1961	2 Sept 1971
October	WAGG, Walter William, *Carpenter's Yard, Sandringham*			
	LINES, William James, *Sandringham, Woods*			

1942

		30 years clasp	40 years clasp	50 years clasp
January	GODFREY, Percy, *Wolferton Farm*	Jan 1952	Jan 1963	Jan 1973
February	YALLOP, George William, *Carpenter's Yard, Sandringham*			

		30 years clasp	40 years clasp	50 years clasp
May	BIGGS, Frederick, *Carpenter's Yard, Sandringham*	4 Feb 1952		
	CROSS, Percy D., *Sandringham, Woods*	12 May 1952		
	DORMAN, Reginald G., *Gardener, Sandringham*	May 1952	15 May 1962	15 May 1972
June	GREENER, Edward V., *Chief Coal Porter*	12 June 1952		
	MORGAN, Horace G., *Sandringham Woods (and Verger, Sandringham Church)*	June 1952	15 June 1962	
July	ANDERSEN, Alex J., *Forestry, Balmoral*	17 July 1952		
August	STUART, Jean, *Housemaid, Windsor Castle*	17 Aug 1952		
	HABGOOD, Victor, *Stovesmith, Superintendent's Staff*	26 Aug 1952		
November	EASTWICK, James Frederick, *Carpenter's Yard, Sandringham*	10 Nov 1952		

1943

		30 years clasp	40 years clasp	50 years clasp
January	JAKEMAN, Leonard, *House Carpenter, Sandringham*	1 Jan 1953	1 Jan 1963	1 Jan 1973
	SYMONS, Mrs Alice, *Seamstress Superintendent's Staff, Sandringham*			
	ALLEN, Alfred, *Carpenter's Yard, Sandringham*	29 Jan 1953	29 Jan 1963	29 Jan 1973
	MITCHELL, Arthur F., *Under Butler* (*It came to light that he was employed at Sandringham from Oct 1918 to 26 Jan 1923, making his qualifying date for the 50 years clasp 30 Sept 1968*)			
	HALL, Charles Edward, *Porter, Royal Pavillion, Aldershot*	3 Feb 1953		
February	PICKEN, Thomas F., *Queen Mary's Household*	5 Feb 1953		
	MITCHELL, Harry (or Henry), *Carpenter's Yard, Sandringham*	Feb 1953		
March	GILDER, George A., *Labourer, Kitchen Garden, Windsor*	1 Mar 1953		
	DANIELS, Stanley E.W., *Carpenter's Yard, Sandringham*	4 Mar 1953		
	EMMERSON, Alfred, *Coal Porter, Sandringham*			
	LINCOLN, Algernon R., *Wolferton Farm*			
April	CROWE, Anthony C., *Carpenter's Yard, Sandringham*	Apr 1953		
	RICHES, James John, *Sandringham Woods*			
	WILLIAMS, Christopher, *Caretaker, Royal Mausoleum*			
	MACLEAN, Catherine, *The Queen's Dresser*			
June	WAGSTAFF, Frank J., *Chauffeur, Royal Mews*			
November	JAMIESON, Alfred A., *Gardener, Balmoral*			
	HANSLIP, Anthony S., *Post Office, Sandringham* (*Started as a boy in the Gardens Mar 1923*)	Mar 1953	1 Mar 1963	
	CAMPBELL, John R., *Joiner, Balmoral*	19 Nov 1953		
	ODLUM, Mrs Edith, *Housemaid, Buckingham Palace*			

1944

		30 years clasp	40 years clasp	50 years clasp
January	HAILEY, Cyril, *Page of the Backstairs*	1 Jan 1954	31 Dec 1963	
	NEWMAN, Leonard J.F., *Queen Mary's Household*			
	SOUTHGATE, Reginald, *Thoroughbred Stud, Sandringham*	Jan 1954	1 Jan 1964	
March	OWEN, Henry, *Stud Groom, Royal Mews*			
	WOOLLEY, Sidney, *Upholsterer, Superintendent's Staff, Buckingham Palace*	23 Mar 1954	23 Mar 1964	
	CATTO, Robert G., *Shepherd, Royal Farms, Windsor*	26 Mar 1954	26 Mar 1964	
	BOYCE, Henry, *Storekeeper, Superintendent's Staff*			
	WADE, George, *Appleton Farm, Sandringham*	10 Mar 1954	10 Mar 1964	
April	ROBERTS, Archibald, *Deputy Foreman, Superintendent's Staff*	12 Apr 1954		
	CLARK, Annie, *Linen Maid, Buckingham Palace*	14 Apr 1954		
	CAMPBELL, James McKay, *Balmoral*			
	BUNN, John, *Sandringham Gardens*	1 Apr 1954		
May	WILLIAMS, Beatrice, *The King's Senior Housemaid*	3 May 1954		
	MCGREGOR, William, *Stalker, Balmoral*	28 May 1954		
August	SOUTHGATE, Frederick S.S., *Chauffeur, Queen Mary's Household*			
October	ROUT, Walter J., *Cabinet Maker, Windsor Castle* (*Time at Carving School, Sandringham, counted. Medal awarded 1950*)	Oct 1954		
	NICOLL, Robert B., *Balmoral*	Oct 1954	17 Oct 1964	
	BIGGS, Leonard, *Appleton Farm*	Oct 1954	1 Oct 1964	1 Oct 1974
November	STEPHEN, Charles H., *Balmoral*	3 Nov 1954		
	JOHNSON, Robert, *Appleton Farm*			

	30 years clasp	40 years clasp	50 years clasp

1945

January	COOK, Charles H., *Head Gardener, Sandringham*			
	BRADSHAW, Frederick, *Upholsterer, Superintendent's Staff Buckingham Palace*			
	BATES, Albert Ernest, *Sandringham*	19 Jan 1955		
March	CHAPMAN, Percy H., *Chauffeur*			
	DISBURY, George Edward, *Assistant. Metal Smith, Superintendent's Staff, Windsor Castle*	2 Mar 1955		
	BUGG, Albert Wilfred, *Carpenter's Yard, Sandringham*			
April	HARLOW, Frank, *Sandringham, Gardens*			
	HART, Hubert, *Upholsterer, Superintendent's Staff, Buckingham Palace*			
	STURGESS, Edward J., *Windsor Royal Gardens*	6 Apr 1955	6 Apr 1965	
	LINSCOT, Mrs Martha, *Daily Help, Royal Mews,*	27 Apr 1955	27 Apr 1965	
May	HUBBARD, H., *Superintendent's Staff, Windsor Castle*	9 May 1955	9 May 1965	9 May 1975
	WILSON, Frederick A., *Foreman, Superintendent's Staff Windsor Castle*			
	CUMPER, Sidney George, *Page, Queen Mary's Household*			
	SAUNDERS, Elizabeth, *Housemaid, Buckingham Palace*	13 May 1955		
June	STEWART, John A., *Senior Footman*	1 June 1955	31 May 1965	
	MORRISON, Donald, *Balmoral*			
	MCGARTHLAND, James, *Balmoral*	29 June 1955	29 June 1965	
July	BROWNE, Benjamin H., *Messenger, Lord Chamberlain's Office*	1 July 1955		
	EMMERTON, Arthur, *Cabinet Maker, Buckingham Palace*	4 July 1955		
August	MOODY, Mrs Edith J., *Temporary Daily Help*	Aug 1955	Aug 1965	
October	STUART, Alexander, *Balmoral*			
	MARRINGTON, Robert C., *Tapissier, Sandringham*	12 Oct 1955	12 Oct 1965	
November	JOHNSON, Sidney George, *Under Butler*	11 Nov 1955	11 Nov 1965	
December	LUCKING, Stanley, *Chief Upholsterer, Windsor Castle*	7 Dec 1955		

1946

January	SMITH, James R., *Royal Paddocks, Hampton Court*			
March	BORLEY, Charles, *Sandringham*			
April	HALL, Thomas J., *Harness Cleaner*	1 Apr 1956		
	HALSE, Arthur, *Upholsterer, Windsor Castle*	19 Apr 1956		
May	PRINGLE, Arthur, *Balmoral*	2 May 1956	2 May 1966	
	DICKIE, John, *Balmoral*	28 May 1956	28 May 1966	
June	STANDALOFT, Harold A., *Sandringham*	5 June 1956		
	SMITH, Frank, *Motor Washer*			
	NEWMAN, Ernest A.G., *Queen Mary's Household*			
August	THATCHER, Reginald G.H., *Upholsterer, Windsor Castle*	14 Aug 1956		
September	MACDONALD, Margaret McKay, *Maid to Princess Elizabeth*	1 Sept 1956	1 Sept 1966	
	DAW, Robert F., *Sandringham*			
	ALLEN, Jack, *Sandringham*	11 Sept 1956		
	AINSLIE, James R.R., *Palace Steward, Buckingham Palace*	27 Sept 1956		
November	FRASER, Alexander, *Balmoral*	1 Nov 1956		
December	CUMMINS, Francis George, *Windsor Royal Farm*			
	NURSE, George William, *Sandringham*	1 Dec 1956		

1947

January	ARNOLD, George, *Driver, Royal Mews*	1 Jan 1957		
	HARKNESS, Jean, *Queen Mary's Second Housemaid*			
	MACDONALD, Barbara, *Housemaid, Windsor Castle*	21 Jan 1957		
	DUNHAM, Jessie May, *Queen Mary's First Dresser*			
February	BROWN, Elizabeth, *Housemaid, Windsor Castle*			
	HUNTER, Walter W., *Sandringham*			
	CALDER, Mrs Elizabeth, *Established Basement Maid, Buckingham Palace*	12 Feb 1957		
	BLAND, Gordon Lane, *Steward's Room Assistant, Marlborough House*			
March	ODLUM, Mrs Edith, *Linen Maid, Buckingham Palace*	1 Mar 1957	1 Mar 1967	
	PRIOR, Albert A., *Clerk to Superintendent, Buckingham Palace*			
	SENTER, Walter R., *Sandringham*			

		30 years clasp	40 years clasp	50 years clasp
	ROSE, Margaret, *Coffee Room Maid, Buckingham Palace* (*Broken service, presented 1949, medal dated 1947; Clasp 1 Jan 1958*)	27 Mar 1957		
April	GODFREY, Robert H.G., *Royal Paddocks, Hampton Court*	1 Apr 1957	1 Apr 1967	
	BENSTEAD, Arthur B., *Cabinet Maker, Windsor Castle* (*Time at Carving School, Sandringham counted. Medal awarded 1950.*)	4 Apr 1957	4 Apr 1967	
May	ATTFIELD, Robert John, *Servant's Hall Assistant, Marlborough House*			
	NIVEN, John, *Balmoral*	23 May 1957		
	MCGREGOR, Elizabeth, *Balmoral (later Princess Elizabeth's Household)*	24 May 1957		
	MCHARDY, Donald, *Stalker, Balmoral*	24 May 1957		
	GIBSON, Charles, *Privy Purse Messenger*	May 1957	1 May 1967	
	WEBBER, Mrs Lilian G., *Temporary Daily Help*	May 1957	1 May 1967	
June	MEADE, Helena, *Housemaid, Buckingham Palace*	16 June 1957	16 June 1967	
July	CHILDS, Stanley, *Page of the Presence and (later) Queen's Page*	10 July 1957	10 July 1967	
September	BRIDGES, Donald, *Sandringham*	1 Sept 1957	1 Sept 1967	
October	GRAY, Mrs Elizabeth, *Coffee Room, Windsor Castle* (*Special award for long non-continuous service.*)			
	HOLMES, Edith, *Housemaid, Windsor Castle*	27 Oct 1957	27 Oct 1967	

1948

February	HOARE, Arthur, *Labourer, Royal Gardens, Windsor*	4 Feb 1958		
	SHURLEY, Henry, *Porter and Caretaker, Frogmore*	11 Feb 1958		
	SHURLEY, William, *Metalsmith, Superintendent's Staff, Windsor Castle*	11 Feb 1958	11 Feb 1968	
	ANNISON, Joseph, *Sandringham*	20 Feb 1958	20 Feb 1968	
	EMMERSON, William J., *Sandringham*	20 Feb 1958	20 Feb 1968	
	JOSLIN, Richard J., *Postillion*	26 Feb 1958		
March	MOORE, Mrs Eliza, *Housekeeper, Marlborough House*			
	WILSON, Douglas W., *Balmoral*			
April	LINTOTT, Lucy, *Housemaid, Windsor Castle*	25 Apr 1958		
May	RUDDLE, Arthur, *Livery Porter, Windsor Castle*			
	HUMPHREY, Bert, *Sandringham*	14 May 1958	14 May 1968	
	HUMPHREY, George, *Sandringham*	14 May 1958	14 May 1968	
	JERRAM, Thomas, *The King's Chief Valet*			
	RAWLINGS, William, *Leading Porter, Superintendent's Staff, Windsor Castle*	19 May 1958	19 May 1968	
June	LEWIN, Reginald R., *Thoroughbred Stud*	26 June 1958		
July	PARK, Mrs Mary E., *Daily Help, Windsor Castle* (*Special award for long non-continuous service*)			
	COOZE, Joseph W., *Established Helper (Driver and Postillion) Royal Mews*	29 July 1958		
October	HURLE, Alfred T., *Head Chauffeur*			
November	STUART, Edwin, *Head Gardener, Balmoral*	7 Nov 1958	7 Nov 1968	
	CAMPBELL, Alexandra, *Housekeeper, Balmoral*	1 Dec 1958		
	STOKOE, Edward, *Forestry, Sandringham*			

1949

January	BAKER, William, *Under Butler, Buckingham Palace*	1 Jan 1959	1 Jan 1969	
March	STRINGER, Albert Edward, *Groom*	1 Mar 1959	1 Mar 1969	
	MACE, Thomas Frank Harold, *Packer, Marlborough House*			
May	EMMERSON, James Robert, *Sandringham*	17 May 1959	17 May 1969	
December	RUTLAND, Frederick A., *Postillion*	1 Dec 1959		
	ABBOTT, George Victor C., *Superintendent's Staff, Buckingham Palace*	7 Dec 1959	7 Dec 1969	
	ROUS, André, *Pastry Cook*	16 Dec 1959	16 Dec 1969	
	BARRETT, Mrs Eleanora, *Daily Help, Buckingham Palace*			
	BARNES, Lily, *Housemaid's Help, Buckingham Palace*			

1950

| January | LAWSON, Maurice Edward, *Superintendent's Staff, Buckingham Palace* | | | |

		30 years clasp	40 years clasp	50 years clasp
February	MANN, Elsie Edith May, *Housemaid, Sandringham*	1 Feb 1960		
March	DAWKINS, Francis William, *Superintendent's Staff, Windsor Castle*	8 Mar 1960		
	HALCOOP, Harold William, *Shoeing Smith*			
	MICHIE, Douglas, *Balmoral*	1 Mar 1960	31 Mar 1970	
April	TRIPP, Albert, *Livery Porter, Buckingham Palace*	12 Apr 1960		
May	DODD, Francis David Thomas, *Page, Buckingham Palace*			
	ANTHONY, Irene Ida, *Cook, Royal Lodge*	7 May 1960	7 May 1970	
	MAYES, Frederick S., *Superintendent's Staff, Buckingham Palace*	10 May 1960		
	JAKEMAN, Grenville C., *Sandringham Gardens*	1 May 1960	1 May 1970	
July	STUNELL, Rosina Rachel, *Housemaid, Buckingham Palace*			
	CREEK, Mabel, *Queen Mary's Second Dresser*			
	MURRAY, Michael W., *Gate Porter, Royal Mews*	13 July 196		
	BROOKES, Mrs Catherine, *Carpet Seamstress, Buckingham Palace*			
August	CRANCHER, Alice Helen, *Housemaid, Windsor Castle*	6 Aug 1960		
September	FERGUSON, Janet Margaret, *Housekeeper, Buckingham Palace*			
October	BARNHAM, Thomas J., *Stores Clerk, Buckingham Palace* (*Still in service on 6 Oct 1960 but having been promoted to Official Grade, he was no longer eligible for 30 years Clasp*)			
	ROBBINS, Harry, *Sandringham*	10 Oct 1960	10 Oct 1970	
	WILLINGHAM, Clifford L., *Sandringham*	11 Oct 1960		
	MITCHELL, Isabella, *Head Housemaid, Balmoral*	19 Oct 1960		
	SHORT, Richard, *Gate Porter, Royal Mews*	19 Oct 1960	19 Oct 1970	
December	TREACY, Carrie, *Nurse, Royal Mews*			
	WELLS, George C., *Sandringham*			

1951

		30 years clasp	40 years clasp	50 years clasp
January	EDWARDS, William, *Carpet Planner, Buckingham Palace*			
	TAYLOR, Cecil Francis, *Cabinet Maker, Buckingham Palace*	3 Jan 1961		
February	POLSON, Marion Mackay, *Head Housemaid in charge of Palace*			
March	SHARP, Edward Arthur James, *Coal Porter, Marlborough House*			
	MILLER, Archibald Thomas Philip, *Watchman, Sandringham*			
April	EVITTS, Reginald John, *Page of the Presence*	1 Apr 1961	1 Apr 1971	
May	HAVERLEY, Maurice F., *Royal Farms, Windsor*			
	BASHAM, Alfred, *Foreman, Sandringham Farm*	29 May 1961		
July	THOW, William, *Balmoral*	1 July 1961	1 July 1971	
	STONE, Reah Lucy, *Housemaid, Windsor Castle*			
	PORTER, William Edward, *Motor Washer, Marlborough House*			
August	BEATTY, William James, *Inventory Clerk, Windsor Castle*	22 Aug 1961		

1952

		30 years clasp	40 years clasp	50 years clasp
January	HARRINGTON, Edgar George, *Footman, Marlborough House and later Page to Queen Mary*			
March	MACDONALD, James Harpur, *Assistant Valet to King (later Valet to Duke of Edinburgh, and at the time of 40 Years Clasp, Valet to Prince of Wales)* (*Medal bearing the effigy of King George VI awarded by the Queen as a special case*)	13 Mar 1962	13 Mar 1972	

1955

		30 years clasp	40 years clasp	50 years clasp
April	HAYWARD, Jon Horace, *Sandringham, (a late award)*			

THE RULES AND REGULATIONS OF THE QUEEN ELIZABETH II LONG AND FAITHFUL SERVICE MEDAL

===

GEORGE R.I.

ELIZABETH THE SECOND, by the Grace of God, of Great Britain, Ireland, and the British Dominions beyond the Seas, Queen, Defender of the Faith, to all whom these Presents shall come,

GREETING!

WHEREAS We have taken into Our Royal Consideration the long and faithful services to Our Person which are being and have been rendered by Our Servants both before and after Our Accession to the Throne.

And whereas We are desirous of distinguishing such service by some mark of Our Royal Favour We do by these Presents for Us institute and create a Medal to be called and known by the name style and designation of the "Queen Elizabeth II Long and Faithful Service Medal" and We are hereby graciously pleased to make ordain and establish the following ordinances for the government of the same.

Firstly: It is ordained that the aforesaid Long and Faithful Service Medal shall be a circular Medal of Silver surmounted by Our Royal Cypher ensigned with a representation of Our Crown having on the obverse Our Royal Effigy and on the reverse, an ornamental design with the words "For Long and Faithful Service" and shall bear on the rim the name of the person upon whom We are pleased to confer the said Medal.

Secondly: It is ordained that the Medal shall be worn on the left breast of the coat or outer garment pendent from a riband of the width of one inch, in dark blue, with three vertical red stripes superimposed, and that in the official list showing the order in which Orders, Decorations and Medals shall be worn it shall be placed immediately after King George the Sixth's Long and Faithful Service Medal.
Provided that when the Medal is worn by a woman, it may be worn on the left shoulder, suspended from a riband of the same width and colour, fashioned into a bow.

Thirdly: It is ordained that the Medal shall only be awarded to those Servants who shall have been for a period of at least twenty years in the service of Our Person, service to Us before Our Accession to the Throne being considered as forming part of the said period, or in the service of Our Royal Father, His late Majesty King George the Sixth, or in the service of Our Royal Grandfather, His late Majesty King George the Fifth, after His Accession to the Throne, or in the service of Her Majesty Queen Elizabeth The Queen Mother, either during the Reign of Our Royal Father or subsequently, or in the service of Our Royal Grandmother, Queen Mary, either during the Reign of Our Royal Grandfather or subsequently, or in the service of His Royal Highness The Duke of Edinburgh since His Royal Highness's Marriage to Us or after Our Accession, or in the service of Our Royal Uncle King Edward the Eighth after his creation as Prince of Wales or after His Accession to the Throne and up to the time of Our Royal Father's Accession, service in any of the aforesaid capacities being aggregated.

Provided that holders of the "Long and Faithful Service Medal" instituted by Our Royal Father, His late Majesty King George the Sixth, or the similar Medal instituted by Our Royal Grandfather, His late Majesty King George the Fifth, shall not be eligible for the Medal instituted by this Our Warrant until they have been at least twenty years in the service of Our Person, or in the service of Her Majesty Queen Elizabeth The Queen Mother, subsequent to the date of Our Accession, or in the service of Our Royal Grandmother, Queen Mary, subsequent to the date of Our Accession, service in the aforesaid capacities being aggregated.

Fourthly: It is ordained that Servants of Our Household or of the Household of Her Majesty Queen Elizabeth The Queen Mother, or of Her Majesty Queen Mary's Household or of His Royal Highness The Duke of Edinburgh's Household who, subsequent to receiving the said Medal instituted by this Our Warrant, shall have completed ten years additional service as defined in the first part of the Third Clause of this Warrant, shall, upon the recommendation of the Keeper of Our Privy Purse, be awarded a Clasp in respect of the said further service, the Clasp to be attached to the riband by which the said Medal is suspended, and shall in respect of every subsequent ten years service be awarded additional Clasps subject nevertheless to Our Royal Sanction in each case.

Fifthly: It is ordained that any Servant of Our Household, or of the Household of Her Majesty Queen Elizabeth The Queen Mother, or of Her Majesty Queen Mary's Household, or of His Royal Highness The Duke of Edinburgh's Household, who has been awarded the "Long and Faithful Service Medal" instituted by Our Royal Father, His late Majesty King George the Sixth, or the similar Medal instituted by Our Royal Grandfather, His late Majesty King George the Fifth, shall in respect of each further ten years additional service as defined in the first part of the Third Clause of this Our Warrant subsequent to the award of such Medal, be eligible for the award of a Clasp to the aforesaid Medal already awarded. The award of a Clasp or Clasps accordingly in respect, partly or wholly, of any service which would be reckoned towards the period of twenty years mentioned in the proviso to the Third Clause of this Our Warrant shall not prevent the reckoning of such service under that proviso.

Sixthly: It is ordained that the Keeper of Our Privy Purse for the time being shall be the custodian of this Our Royal Warrant and shall from time to time submit for Our consideration the names of such Servants as may be eligible to receive the said Medal and Clasps, and further, shall keep a Register of the names of those upon whom We may be pleased to confer this Medal.

Seventhly: It is ordained that upon the death of a recipient of the said Medal the latter shall remain in the possession of such recipient's representatives, no person however being entitled to wear the said Medal.

Eighthly: It is ordained that reproductions of the Long and Faithful Service Medal, known as a Miniature Medal, which may be worn on certain occasions by those to whom the Medal is awarded, shall be half the size of the Long and Faithful Service Medal.

Ninthly: It is ordained that if any Servant upon whom We have been pleased to confer the Medal shall be guilty of such conduct as in the judgement of Us, Our Heirs and Successors, disqualifies such Servant from continuing to wear the same, the Medal shall be forfeited, and the name of the Servant shall be forthwith erased from the Register of those upon whom the said Medal shall have been conferred: provided that it shall be competent for Us, Our Heirs and Successors to restore the Medal so forfeited.

Given at Our Court at St. James's the twenty-sixth day of January, 1953, in the first year of Our Reign.

By Her Majesty's Command,

Tryon,
Keeper of the Privy Purse.

RECIPIENTS OF
THE QUEEN ELIZABETH II
LONG AND FAITHFUL
SERVICE MEDAL

―

		30 years clasp	40 years clasp	50 years clasp
1952				
April	EMMERSON, Reginald William, *Bricklayer, Sandringham*	18 Apr 1962	18 Apr 1972	
May	HAWKINS, Gilbert, *Polisher, Windsor Castle*	14 May 1962		
June	DAVIES, Meredith Vaughan, *Clerk to Superintendent Windsor Castle*			
	RITCHIE, Edgar V., *Royal Farms, Windsor*			
July	BROWN, Rupert Urquhart, *Ghillie, Balmoral*	1 July 1962		
	ALLAN, Alfred Junior, *House Foreman, Marlborough House*			
August	ROBLUE, Stanley Wilfred, *Messenger, Lord Chamberlain's Office*	22 Aug 1962	22 Aug 1972	
September	FORSYTH, David S., *Royal Farms, Windsor (later Long Walk Gatekeeper*	14 Sept 1962		
	FRY, Walter Robin, *First Assistant Plate Pantry, Buckingham Palace*	26 Sept 1962		
October	WILES, Albert George, *Rough Rider, Royal Mews*	1 Oct 1962		
November	BACON, Laurence Alfred, *Yeoman of the Silver Pantry, Marlborough House*			
	OULTON, Charles, *Serjeant Footman (later Palace Steward)*	19 Nov 1962		
December	BURKITT, Edwin John, *Carriage Overseer, Royal Mews*	1 Dec 1962		
1953				
January	FORSYTH, James, *Royal Farms, Windsor (Awarded 30 Years Clasp as a special case. Left service 2 Nov 1962)*	23 Oct 1962		
March	ROBSON, William, *Serjeant Farrier, Royal Mews*			
	FELLOWS, Miss Alice Winifred, *Upholstress, Windsor Castle*			
	MORGAN, Arthur William, *Sandringham*			
April	SMITH, Robert Charles, *Deputy Serjeant Footman*	1 Apr 1963		
	MARTIN, Stanley Louis, *Assistant Inventory Clerk, Buckingham Palace*	22 Apr 1963		
	MCGREGOR, James, *Balmoral*			
July	GOODSHIP, William C., *Sandringham*	1 July 1963		
September	JONES, Richard, *Poultryman, Royal Farms, Windsor*			
October	TILLEY, Frank John, *Polisher, Superintendent's Staff, Windsor Castle*	14 Oct 1963	14 Oct 1973	
November	SCOTT, Walter, *Balmoral*			
	MACKENZIE, Miss Barbara, *Housekeeper, Birkhall*			
1954				
January	PAICE, Stanley A., *Stove and Flue Attendant, Superintendent's Staff, Buckingham Palace*	1 Jan 1964	1 Jan 1974	
February	BOWMAN, Robert H., *Sandringham*	1 Feb 1964	1 Jan 1974	
	COLLINS, William, *Caretaker, St James's Palace*			
	GORDON, Mrs Robina J., *Princess Margaret's Dresser*			
	BENHAM, Percy, *Yeoman of the Glass and China Pantry*	23 Feb 1964	23 Feb 1974	
	PARKES, James, *Postillion, Royal Mews*			
March	CLARK, William, *Sandringham*			
April	DAY, Ernest A., *Binder, Royal Library*	16 Apr 1964	16 Apr 1974	
	BISSET, Hugh, *Balmoral*			
	COLEMAN, Kathleen M., *Second Linen Maid, Buckingham Palace*			
October	EAST, Walter E., *HM Thoroughbred Stud*	6 Oct 1964		
November	WEDDLE, Alexander, *Royal Mews*	4 Nov 1964		

		30 years clasp	40 years clasp	50 years clasp
December	SMITH, Albert E., *Page of the Presence (with Queen Mary 1936–53)*	1 Dec 1964	1 Dec 1974	

1955

January	GRIST, Alfred E., *Sandringham*	1 Jan 1965	1 Jan 1975	
	PREECE, Arthur V., *Postillion, Royal Mews (later Livery Porter, St James's Palace)*	1 Jan 1965	1 Jan 1975	
February	MACKAY, George, *Balmoral*	4 Feb 1965		
April	MILLS, Mrs Edith E., *Daily Help, Lord Chamberlain's Department* (entered service 1926)			
August	PEARCE, Ernest, *Oddman, Royal Lodge*	6 Aug 1965		
September	TATE, Muriel Alice, *Coffee Room Maid*	9 Sept 1965		
	SMITH, Elsie Constance, *Housemaid, Windsor Castle*	10 Sept 1965		
December	NICHOLSON, Walter Gerald, *Livery Porter, Windsor Castle*	1 Dec 1965		

1956

January	COOK, Cecil, *Messenger, Lord Chamberlain's Office*			
	WARD, Hilda, *Housemaid, Buckingham Palace*	1 Jan 1966		
April	COLLINSON, Arthur, *Sandringham*			
July	GILL, Joseph K., *Caretaker, Chapel Royal, Hampton Court*	21 July 1966		
August	MACDONALD, Robert G., *Oddman, Royal Lodge*	1 Aug 1966	1 Aug 1976	
	TACK, Charles J., *Table Decker, Royal Gardens, Windsor*	1 Aug 1966	1 Aug 1976	
	WADE, Florence, *Housemaid, Windsor Castle (later Housekeeper, Sandringham)*	1 Aug 1966		
	BARFOOT, Mrs Nellie F., *Basement Maid, Buckingham Palace*			
September	NORMAN, Ada, *Housemaid, Buckingham Palace*			
October	ALLCOCK, Henry C., *Sandringham*			
	BENTLEY, Frank, *Livery Porter, Buckingham Palace*	19 Oct 1966		
	TAYLOR, Walter, *Footman to Queen Elizabeth the Queen Mother (later Steward, Clarence House)*	19 Oct 1966	19 Oct 1976	
	BALFOUR, William, *Storeman, Royal Mews* (*Died before presentation; medal sent to widow by command of The Queen*)			
November	HARWOOD, Alfred, *Leading Porter, Superintendent's Staff Buckingham Palace*	16 Nov 1966		
December	CLARKE, Harold, *State Room Porter, Windsor Castle*	7 Dec 1966		
	SUGG, Eric, *Upholsterer, Windsor Castle*			
	SERGY, Montague, *Head Privy Purse Messenger* (*formerly with Palace Police for 19 years*)			

1957

January	CHRISTIE, Francis, *Balmoral*			
	JONES, Gethyn, *Stove and Flue Attendant Buckingham Palace*	30 Jan 1967		
February	BENSTEAD, John, *Sandringham*	1 Feb 1967		
	DODD, Edward, *Sandringham*			
March	WHITING, Frederick F., *Under Butler (later Yeoman of the Wine Cellars)*	15 Mar 1967	15 Mar 1977	
	GODFREY, George Laurence, *Sandringham*	19 Mar 1967	19 Mar 1977	19 Mar 1987
	THOROGOOD, Frederick G., *Page of the Presence*			
April	BAKER, Arthur, *Usher, Steward's Room*	10 Apr 1967	10 Apr 1977	
	ATHOW, Peter C., *Carpenter's Yard, Sandringham*	24 Apr 1967	24 Apr 1977	24 Apr 1987
	AUBERY, Ronald H., *Head Cook, Royal Kitchen*	27 Apr 1967		
May	GILLAN, James, *Balmoral*	27 May 1967		
June	GILLSON, Miss Kathleen, *Bothy Attendant, Sandringham*			
July	DAW, Raymond W. J., *Sandringham Gardens*	3 July 1967	3 July 1977	
August	SMITH, Norah, *Head Coffee Room Maid*			
	BRAND, Morton H., *Royal Gardens, Windsor*			
	CROWE, Cyril J., *Sandringham*	27 Aug 1967	27 Aug 1977	27 Aug 1987
	PARMITER, Wilfred E.B., *Sandringham*			
October	ROBERTSON, Margaret, *Housemaid and Caretaker, Abergeldie Castle*			
	KEMBLE, Miss Irene A.M., *Clarence House*			
	CLARK, John Edward, *Sandringham Game Department*	15 Oct 1967	15 Oct 1977	15 Oct 1987
	BRINKLEY, Cecil C., *Royal Gardens, Windsor*	16 Oct 1967		

		30 years clasp	40 years clasp	50 years clasp
November	BAILEY, Edward G., *Royal Farms, Windsor*	12 Nov 1967		
	DODD, Edward A., *Sandringham, Game Department*	26 Nov 1967		

1958

		30 years clasp	40 years clasp	50 years clasp
February	WATT, James, *Balmoral Estate (Broken service)*	3 Aug 1968		
March	JONES, Ann Ellen, *Housekeeper, Staff of Queen Elizabeth The Queen Mother*	1 Mar 1968	1 Mar 1978	
April	OSMOND, Owen Thomas, *Storekeeper, Superintendent's Staff, Buckingham Palace*			
	GORDON, George, *Balmoral*	4 Apr 1968		
May	COOZE, Walter, *Harness Cleaner, Royal Mews*	16 May 1968	16 May 1978	
June	FORBES, James McGregor, *Sandringham Gardens*	6 June 1968		
July	WADDLING, Florence, *Housemaid, Buckingham Palace*			
October	JAMES, David Albert, *Gate Porter, Royal Mews*			
November	YOUNG, James, *Balmoral (formerly at Abergeldie for 6½ years)*	28 May 1972		
December	BOCKING, Ernest Walter, *Sandringham*			
	LONG, Alfred Ernest, *Postillion, Royal Mews*	20 Dec 1968		

1959

		30 years clasp	40 years clasp	50 years clasp
January	FARROW, Bernard Eric, *Sandringham Gardens*	16 Jan 1969	16 Jan 1979	16 Jan 1989
February	RICHES, Leonard Horace, *Kitchen Porter (later Livery Porter, Buckingham Palace)*	1 Feb 1969		
	MINDHAM, Frederick George, *Appleton Gardens, Sandringham*			
	HARROD, Leslie Arthur, *Sandringham Fire Station*			
March	BORLEY, Rose Mary, *Housemaid, Windsor Castle (Broken Service, later Mrs Crowe, Daily Help at Sandringham*	1 Jan 1977		
April	MELTON, Maurice, *Sandringham Game Department*	21 Apr 1969	21 Apr 1979	
May	WOOD, Herbert Thorpe Warwick, *Second Chauffeur, Royal Mews (later Livery Porter, subsequently Page)*	14 May 1969	14 May 1979	
	BREWER, Jack Arthur, *Superintendent's Staff, Windsor Castle*	22 May 1969		
	FREEMAN, Charles William, *Royal Farms, Windsor*			
July	APPLEBY, John Richard, *Head Messenger, Privy Purse*			
	WALTON, James Edward, *Page of the Presence*	24 July 1969		
	CUFF, Leonard Walter, *Canteen Assistant and Storekeeper*	27 July 1969		
August	HATCHER, Ernest George, *Groom, Royal Mews, Windsor*	21 Aug 1969		
October	BRUCE, Mrs Alice Jane, *Housekeeper, Windsor Castle*			
November	EVANS, Margaret Ann, *Head Linen Maid, Windsor Castle*			

1960

		30 years clasp	40 years clasp	50 years clasp
January	HAIMES, Sidney Samuel, *Store Clerk, Buckingham Palace*			
	JAMES, Mrs Jane, *Daily Help, Royal Mews (Broken service)*			
	MORRISON, Donald, *Store Clerk, Buckingham Palace*			
	MALAN, Jean-Pierre, *Staff Cook, Buckingham Palace*	1 Jan 1970		
	VINCETT, Leonard Francis Lee, *Store Clerk, Buckingham Palace*	1 Jan 1970		
February	SHERIDAN, Bertha, *Housekeeper, Frogmore House*			
March	HAVERS, George Herbert, DCM, *Steward, Royal Lodge, Windsor*			
	STOKOE, George William Henry, *Sandringham*	28 Mar 1970		
May	CANDY, Charles Alexander, *Deputy Serjeant Footman*	28 May 1970	28 May 1980	
June	TUTT, Cecily Winifred, *Housemaid, Buckingham Palace*			
	PATRICK, Frederick Owen, *Sandringham*			
July	BANNOCHIE, William Greig, *Clerk to the Superintendent, Buckingham Palace*			
	DEAL, Harold, *Steward's Room Assistant, Buckingham Palace*			
August	PAGE, Peter Ernest, *Cook, Royal Kitchens, Buckingham Palace (Broken service)*	21 Nov 1982		
	GARNHAM, Frank, *Under Butler, Royal Lodge, Windsor*			
	GYNGELL, Mrs Elizabeth Annie, *Daily Help, Windsor Castle*			
October	GOODSHIP, Douglas Alan, *Post Office, Sandringham (later Sandringham Repairs Department)*	1 Oct 1970	1 Oct 1980	1 Oct 1990
December	DICKMAN, Cyril Sidney, *Senior Footman, (later Palace Steward)*	14 Dec 1970	14 Dec 1980	9 Feb 1990

		30 years clasp	40 years clasp	50 years clasp

1961

February	MACDONALD, Margaret, *Housemaid, Windsor Castle*			
March	ROSS, Miss Isabel Gettins, *Second Dresser*			
July	HARRIS, Leslie, *First Assistant, Servants' Hall, Buckingham Palace (Joined 1919; Broken service.)*			
August	RUMSEY, William, *Royal Farms, Windsor*			
October	ALLEN, Denis Ivor, *Post Office, Sandringham*	1 Oct 1971	1 Oct 1981	
	MONTGOMERY, Arthur, *Royal Farms, Windsor*	1 Oct 1971		
	RIX, Fred, *Sandringham*			
November	JOBLING, Miss Winifred E.A., *Daily Help, Windsor Castle*			

1962

March	DAVIDSON, John, *Balmoral Estate*	23 Mar 1972	23 Mar 1982	
July	PREECE, Norma Ivy Minnie, *Linen Maid, Windsor Castle*			
October	MCSWEENEY, Reginald Anthony, *Privy Purse Messenger*			
December	JONES, Miss Olive, *Cook Housekeeper, Bothy, Royal Gardens, Windsor*			

1963

October	STANLEY, Elsie Vine, *Housemaid, Buckingham Palace*			

1964

January	HUCKSTEP, Mrs Alice Rose, *Housemaid, Buckingham Palace (Joined 1 Feb 1927, broken service.)*			
April	OLIVER, Emily Edith, *Housemaid, Windsor Castle*			
May	GENT, Albert Edward, *Sandringham Farm*			
November	REED, Gilbert Frederick, *Sandringham*	20 Nov 1974	20 Nov 1984	
	HOOKS, Henry, *Sandringham*			
	GILLS, Alexander George, *Royal Farms, Windsor*			

1965

February	TAYLOR, John Errick, *Serjeant Footman, later the Queen's Page*	12 Feb 1975		
March	HEUSTON, Herbert Oliver, *Sandringham Game Department*	23 Mar 1965		
May	HANSLIP, Clifford Walter, *Sandringham, Repairs Department*	16 May 1965		
July	MOODY, Frederick, *Sandringham, Game Department*	18 July 1965		
September	MACDONALD, Alexander, *The Queen's Piper and Page of the Presence*	1 Sept 1965		
October	BROWN, James, *Head Forester, Sandringham*	11 Oct 1965		
November	RYAN, Miss Hannah, *Housemaid, Buckingham Palace*	8 Nov 1965		
	CLOUTING, Albert Edward, *Chauffeur to Queen Elizabeth The Queen Mother*	18 Nov 1965		

1966

January	AMOS, Robert James, *Sandringham Estate*	9 Jan 1976		
	PAINTER, Philip Bryan, *Sandringham*			
February	COLLISON, Leslie Herbert James, *Sandringham*			
	SCOTT, Edward John, *Sandringham*			
	HUISH, Frederick Thomas, *Helper, Royal Mews*			
	GANNON, Frank, *Coal Porter, Buckingham Palace*			
March	DONOGHUE, Michael Silvester, *Polisher, Superintendent's Staff, Buckingham Palace*			
April	PEARCE, Mary Anne Whitfield, *Staff of Queen Elizabeth The Queen Mother (Joined service of King George VI on 1 Apr 1946.)*	1 Apr 1976		
May	BROWN, Ellis Francis, *Sandringham Gardens*			
	PEARCE, Joseph Matthew, *Second Valet to the Duke of Edinburgh*	8 May 1976		
June	EMMERSON, Leonard Arthur, *Sandringham Farms*	26 June 1976		

		30 years clasp	40 years clasp	50 years clasp
July	NICOL, Robertina, *Housemaid, Windsor Castle*	6 July 1976		
	TAYLOR, William Charles, *Royal Mews, Buckingham Palace*			
August	ASPDEN, Thomas, *Second Cook, Royal Kitchens*			
September	METCALFE, Alec Frederick, *Page of the Presence*			
November	BELL, Mrs Gladys Mary, *Housemaid, Buckingham Palace*			
December	MACE, Dennis Stanley, *Sandringham*	11 Dec 1976	11 Dec 1986	

1967

		30 years clasp	40 years clasp	50 years clasp
January	MAY, John William, *Superintendent's Staff, Buckingham Palace (Broken service)*			
	WHINCUP, David James, *Gilder, Superintendent's Staff, Windsor Castle*	4 Jan 1977	4 Jan 1987	
	SMITH, Frank, *Sandringham*	15 Jan 1977	15 Jan 1988	
February	HOOKS, John Ernest, *Sandringham* (*Completed 19 yrs and 11 months before leaving service. Due date would have been 5 Mar 1967.*)			
March	WEBSTER, Alexander, *Balmoral Estate* (*30 year Clasp as Handyman and Gardener on Queen ElizabethThe Queen Mother's Staff, Castle of Mey.*)	31 Mar 1977	31 Mar 1987	31 Mar 1997
April	JENKINS, Glanwyn, *Staff of Queen Elizabeth The Queen Mother* (*Entered service of Queen Mary 1 Apr 1947.*)	1 Apr 1977	1 Apr 1987	
July	SIMMONS, Leslie Robert, *Sandringham*	2 July 1977	2 July 1987	
	HILLIER, Leslie Donald, *Messenger Central Chancery* (*Broken service*)			
September	BUCKINGHAM, Charles William Ernest, *Sandringham*	Sept 1977		
October	FARROW, Ernest John, *Sandringham*			
	FARROW, Fernley Redvers, *Sandringham*	13 Oct 1977		
November	PETRIE, Arthur, *Sandringham*	11 Nov 1977	11 Nov 1987	
December	SECKER, Walter James, *Sandringham*			

1968

		30 years clasp	40 years clasp	50 years clasp
January	JONES, Miss Susan, *Leading Upholsteress, Superintendent's Staff, Buckingham Palace*			
February	DYE, Robert Henry, *Sandringham Woods*	4 Feb 1978		
March	MITCHELL, Frederick William, *Under Butler Buckingham Palace*	9 Mar 1978	9 Mar 1988	
May	WILSON, Archibald, *Balmoral Estate*			
June	LOOSE, Peter Edward, *Sandringham House*	23 June 1978	23 June 1988	
July	FARROW, Melville Gordon, *Sandringham Fruit Farm*	1 July 1978	1 July 1988	
August	WAITE, Frederick George, *Sandringham Gardens* (*later Head Gardener*)	4 Aug 1978	4 Aug 1988	
	WINKWORTH, William George, *Royal Gardens, Windsor*			
September	GLENNIE, James, *Balmoral*			
October	DAVIDSON, Charles Duncan, *Balmoral Estates*	25 Oct 1978	25 Oct 1988	
December	ANDERSON, Miss Mabel, *Head Nursery Maid, Buckingham Palace (with the Queen as Princess Elizabeth)*	15 Dec 1978		

1969

		30 years clasp	40 years clasp	50 years clasp
January	ROBERTSON, Ernest, *Packer, Superintendent's Staff, Buckingham Palace (Broken service)*			
	SKEET, Clifford Bassett, *Steward, Royal Lodge, (Broken service)*	1 Jan 1979		
	HOLLOWAY, William, *Duke of Edinburgh's Page*			
February	PEARL, James, *Balmoral*			
March	WRIGHT, Charles Alexander, *Balmoral*	1 Mar 1979		
	KIRBY, Miss Cecily Frances Louise, *Housemaid, Windsor Castle (Broken service)*			
	ROBINSON, Miss Ruby, *Housemaid, Windsor Castle (Broken service)*			
May	WADE, Mrs Doris Lily, *Sandringham Farm*			
	BENNETT, Ernest, *Page of the Backstairs (The Queen's Page)*			
	ANDERSON, Robert, *Balmoral*	28 May 1979		
	TINSON, William George, *Superintendent's Staff, Windsor Castle (Broken service)*			

		30 years clasp	40 years clasp	50 years clasp
June	BUTLER, Frederick Thomas, *Royal Farms, Windsor*			
August	HARDY, Lawrence, *Upholsterer, Superintendent's Staff, Windsor Castle*	20 Aug 1979	20 Aug 1989	
September	BRAYNE, Walter George, *Leading Porter, Buckingham Palace*	6 Sept 1979		
October	LONG, Herbert Edward, *Page of the Presence*	1 Oct 1979		
November	DUDDIGAN, Edward, *Glass and China Pantry*			

1970

		30 years clasp	40 years clasp	50 years clasp
January	LEGG, Robert William, *Livery Porter*			
April	LINES, David Rodney, *Sandringham Woods*			
May	PURVEY, Harold Arthur, *Head Chauffeur*	7 May 1980		
	BERRESFORD, Stanley Edward, *Mechanic and Tractor Driver, Royal Gardens, Windsor*	20 May 1980		
June	MCCOMBIE, Noel, *Balmoral Estate*	26 June 1980		
July	SMITH, Maurice George, *Sous Chef, Buckingham Palace*	6 July 1980		
	O'HAGAN, Dennis, *Royal Farms, Windsor* (*30 year Clasp given on retirement.*)	5 Feb 1980		
August	BRIDGES, Raymond Frederick, *Motor Engineer, Sandringham*	1 Aug 1980	1 Aug 1990	
October	KENDLE, Arthur William, *Sandringham Farm*			

1971

		30 years clasp	40 years clasp	50 years clasp
March	TALLON, William John Stephenson, *Queen Elizabeth The Queen Mother's Page (later Steward)*	19 Mar 1981	19 Mar 1991	
April	STREAMER, Thomas, *Queen Elizabeth The Queen Mother's Staff*			
	CONROY, Bridget, *Queen Elizabeth The Queen Mother's Staff (Broken service)*	18 Apr 1981		
June	ABEL, Charles A., *Balmoral*			
	WISE, David William, *Assistant, Steward's Room and Staff Dining Room, Buckingham Palace*	25 June 1981		
November	COONEY, Bartholomew, *State Room Porter, Buckingham Palace*			
December	LEITCH, John A. M., *Balmoral Estates*			

1972

		30 years clasp	40 years clasp	50 years clasp
January	TURNER, Patricia Loretto, *Senior Housemaid, Windsor Castle*	1 Jan 1982		
March	MOORES, Eric David, *Tractor Driver, Royal Farms, Windsor*	1 Mar 1982		
May	DONOGHUE, Miss Pamela Mary, *Groom, Royal Mews, Windsor* (*In the employ of Duke of Edinburgh 1952–72, later transferred to the Queen's service to look after Prince of Wales's polo ponies.*)	9 May 1982		
June	HUCKLE, Clarence William, *Wolferton Farm, Sandringham*			
July	FLETCHER, Victor, *Yeoman of the Plate Pantry*	7 July 1982		
August	FARROW, David Hugh, *Sandringham Farms*	1 Aug 1982	1 Aug 1992	
	GAUGHAN, Norman, *Royal Gardens, Windsor*			
November	CAMERON, James, *Keeper at Castle of Mey*			
	BORRETT, Edward, *Royal Farms, Windsor*			

1973

		30 years clasp	40 years clasp	50 years clasp
January	GODFREY, Ernest Richard Thomas, *Wolferton Farm, Sandringham*			
	GRUBB, Andrew, *State Room Porter, Palace of Holyroodhouse*			
February	BUSHELL, George William, *Motor Engineer, Sandringham*	2 Feb 1983		
	SEALEY, Michael Christopher Martin, *Chef, Queen Elizabeth The Queen Mother's Staff*	10 Feb 1983	10 Feb 1993	
	DENT, Miss Pauline Patricia, now Mrs Stanley, *Leading Upholsteress, Buckingham Palace*	16 Feb 1983	16 Feb 1993	

		30 years clasp	40 years clasp	50 years clasp
March	MCRORIE, Robert Collie, *Queen Elizabeth The Queen Mother's Staff*			
	COOKE, Terence Edward, *Queen Elizabeth The Queen Mother's Staff*			
	ROBERTSON, John Begg, BEM, *Stalker, Balmoral*	30 Mar 1983		
April	CARROLL, Patrick, *Messenger, Lord Chamberlain's Office*	13 Apr 1983	13 Apr 1993	
	KENNY, Miss Mary, *Head Housemaid, Queen Elizabeth The Queen Mother's Staff*	17 Apr 1983		
June	LIPSCOMBE, Donald, *Royal Gardens, Windsor*	22 June 1983		
August	CHAPPELL, Derek Charles, *Senior Conservation Officer, Lord Chamberlain's Office*	1 Aug 1983		
	VINCENT, James, *Senior Conservation Officer, Lord Chamberlain's Office*			
	SADLER, Ashley John, *Motor Engineer, Sandringham*	4 Aug 1983	4 Aug 1993	
	PAINTER, Brian Ephriam, *Repairs Department, Sandringham*			
	PARNELL, Anthony Vernon, *Repairs Department, Sandringham*	12 Aug 1983	12 Aug 1993	
October	STEVENS, Ernest Albert, *Game Department, Sandringham*			
November	GALBRAITH, Thomas, *Foreman, Royal Gardens, Windsor*	16 Nov 1983		
	BATES, Frederick Henry George, *Queen Elizabeth The Queen Mother's Staff*			
December	PANKS, Miss Doris Irene, *Senior Housemaid (Linen) Sandringham*	7 Dec 1973		

1974

		30 years clasp	40 years clasp	50 years clasp
January	BADGER, Edward, *Queen Elizabeth The Queen Mother's Staff, Royal Lodge*			
March	CALLENDER, Alexander, QGM *First Chauffeur, Royal Mews*			
	O'DWYER, Miss Mary, *Head Housemaid, Buckingham Palace*			
April	WILSON, Mrs Robina, *Housekeeper, Balmoral Castle*			
May	HARRISON, Henry Edward, *Deputy Head Chauffeur, Royal Mews*	3 May 1984		
November	POLLARD, Thomas, *Royal Farms, Windsor*			
December	WILSON, Miss Julia Mary, *Queen Elizabeth The Queen Mother's Staff*			

1975

		30 years clasp	40 years clasp	50 years clasp
January	WATSON, William Harold, *Superintendent of the Royal Collection, Hampton Court*			
February	NUNN, Arthur Jeffrey, *Game Department, Sandringham*	7 Feb 1985		
March	LINSLEY, Norman, *Senior Liveried Helper, Royal Mews (Broken service)*			
	HUDSON, William, *Coachman, Royal Mews (Broken service)*			
May	MATHESON, James, *Queen Elizabeth The Queen Mother's Staff*			
September	KEMP, Andrew Littlejohn, *Balmoral Estates*	12 Sept 1985	12 Sept 1995	
October	DORAN, Miss Mary, *Queen Elizabeth The Queen Mother's Staff*	24 Oct 1985	24 Oct 1995	
November	OATES, Alfred Francis, *Rough Rider, Royal Mews*	21 Nov 1985	21 Nov 1995	
December	HOPWOOD, Mrs Henriette Cecilia, *Carpet Seamstress Buckingham Palace*			
	BROWN, Mrs Beatrice Ansley, *Queen Elizabeth The Queen Mother's Staff*			

1976

		30 years clasp	40 years clasp	50 years clasp
January	MASON, William Robin, *Royal Farms, Windsor*			
	SADD, Richard James, *Head Messenger, Lord Chamberlain's Office*			
March	DUFF, Thomas Newton, *Balmoral*			
	FIELD, Miss Ivy Gwendoline, *Dresser to Queen Elizabeth The Queen Mother*			

		30 years clasp	40 years clasp	50 years clasp
April	OATES, David Alfred, *Non-Liveried Helper, Royal Mews* (*Broken service*)	15 Apr 1986		
May	WILCOCK, Reginald, *Footman, Queen Elizabeth The Queen Mother's Staff (later Page of the Backstairs)*	10 May 1986	10 May 1996	
	FANCOURT, Edward George, *Senior Conservation Officer*	1 June 1986		
July	WOOD, John Kenneth, *Sous Chef*			
	HOLLAND, Francis Albert, *Travelling Yeoman*	30 July 1986		
November	COLEMAN, Miss Margaret Rachel, *Senior Housemaid, Buckingham Palace*	24 Nov 1986		
December	BARNARD, Albert John, *Sandringham Repairs Department*	26 Sept 1986		

1977

January	COLLINGS, Mrs Edith Wilhelmina, *Queen Elizabeth The Queen Mother's Staff (Broken service)*			
	BIGGS, Christopher Frederick, *Estate Yard, Sandringham*	2 Jan 1987	2 Jan 1997	
	BUSH, Miss Betty, *Senior Housemaid, Windsor Castle*	29 Jan 1987		
February	JARRED, Anthony John, *Deputy Page of the Chambers*	25 Feb 1987		
March	CRANSTON, Frank Samuel, *Luggage Porter, Buckingham Palace*	1 Mar 1987		
April	HAMPSON, Charles Vincent, *Livery Porter, Buckingham Palace*			
	HARROD, Graham John, *Estate Yard, Sandringham*	15 Apr 1987	15 Apr 1997	
	DAY, Richard Laurence, *Binder, Royal Library, Windsor*			
August	GOODMAN, Peter Magnus, *Clerk, Royal Mews Department*			
October	FARROW, Peter Colin, *Sandringham Farms*	16 Oct 1987	16 Oct 1997	
December	GOODWIN, Mrs Phyllis Dorothy, *Daily Help, Royal Mews, Windsor* (*21 yrs service on retirement.*)			

1978

January	JACKSON, James Leonard, *Senior Conservation Officer*	1 Jan 1988	1 Jan 1998	
	NURSE, Ronald Olin, *Sandringham Farm*	31 Jan 1988		
April	MACE, Trevor, *Sandringham Estate Yard*	9 Apr 1988	9 Apr 1998	
	ROBINSON, Mrs Sylvia Joan, *Leading Upholstress, Windsor Castle*			
	NURSE, James Robert, *Assistant, Royal Cellars*			
May	WATTS, David John, *Sandringham Estate Yard*	13 May 1988	13 May 1998	
	MURPHY, Edward George, *Livery Porter (Broken service), formerly First Chauffeur*			
June	EWAN, James Thomas, *Balmoral Estates*	16 June 1988		
July	BUSHELL, Bernard Roy, *Sandringham Woods*	21 July 1988		
October	BARBER, Arthur, *Sandringham Farms*			
	SEAMAN, Ernest William, *Sandringham Farms*			
	WOOD-MURRAY, Mrs Margaret Johanna, *Housemaid, Balmoral Castle*			
November	SCALLAN, Frederick Charles, *Stud Groom, Sandringham*			
	GORDON, Miss Mabel, *Housekeeper, Birkhall*			

1979

April	BIGGS, David Leonard, *Sandringham Estate Yard*	8 Apr 1989		
June	PERRY, Michael, *Page of the Presence*			
July	ROSS, John Walter, *Stockman/Tractorman, Longoe Farm Queen Elizabeth The Queen Mother's Staff*			
August	HAMILTON, Robert Gray, *Yeoman of the Glass and China Pantry*	17 Aug 1989	17 Aug 1999	
September	POLLARD, James Leslie, *Foreman Cabinet Maker Palace of Holyroodhouse*	21 Sept 1989		
	CLARK, Miss Catherine, *Housemaid, Clarence House, Queen Elizabeth The Queen Mother's Staff*			
November	HOATH, Miss Peggy Gladys, *Assistant Dresser to The Queen*	1 Nov 1989		
	ALLINGTON, Raymond, *Sandringham Woods Department*	5 Nov 1989	5 Nov 1999	

		30 years clasp	40 years clasp	50 years clasp
1980				
January	BRYANT, Miss Gertrude Beatrice, *Queen Elizabeth The Queen Mother's Staff*	4 Jan 1990		
February	HOWLING, Roy Thomas William, *Sandringham Farms*	8 Feb 1990		
March	ROSS, John Grassick, *Balmoral*			
April	BOLAND, Richard Charles, *Coachman, Royal Mews*	27 Apr 1990		
May	BUTLER, James Anthony, *Carriage Washer and Harness Cleaner, Royal Mews*	2 May 1990		
	SIMMONS, Abel, *Wolferton Stud*			
	MACKINNON, Sheila Annabel, *Head Housemaid, Windsor Castle (Broken service)*			
July	JUFFS, James Dennis, *Royal Farms, Windsor*			
August	SIMMONS, Colin John, *Sandringham Woods*	15 Aug 1990		
October	MANN, Lionel Thomas, *Sous Chef*	15 Oct 1990		
December	BENEFER, Frederick George, *Sandringham Fruit Farm*	22 Dec 1990	22 Dec 2000	
1981				
January	BAILEY, Kenneth George, *Tractor Driver, Royal Gardens, Windsor*	2 Jan 1991		
	RITCHIE, Cecil John, *Labourer, Works Department, Balmoral Estates*	4 Jan 1991		
	HANSLIP, Mrs Elizabeth Mary, *Part-time Office Cleaner, Sandringham, (Entered service 1946; awarded on retirement.)*			
February	BATTERBEE, Leslie David, *Repair Department Royal Stud*	15 Feb 1991		
March	BAIN, Miss Christina Margaret, *Coffee Room Maid*	24 Mar 1991		
April	WATTS, Maurice John, *Messenger, Lord Chamberlain's Office, Groom of the Vestry*			
	SMITH, Gerald George, *Estate Yard, Sandringham*			
August	CARPENTER, Mrs Eva May, *Upholstress, Industrial Staff, Windsor Castle*			
December	WOODWARD, William Albert, *Palace Attendant, Windsor Castle*			
1982				
January	PRESTON, John, *Carpet Planner, Windsor Castle*	1 Jan 1992		
February	BRYANT, Miss Muriel Bertha, *Housemaid, Royal Lodge, Queen Elizabeth The Queen Mother's Staff*	12 Feb 1992		
	MICKLEBURGH, Edward Cecil, *Sandringham Woods*			
March	WEBSTER, Mrs Maria June Tawse, *Housekeeper, Castle of Mey, Queen Elizabeth The Queen Mother's Staff*		31 March 1996	
April	BROWN, John Alan, *Sandringham Farm*	25 April 1992		
	GODFREY, Philip Roy, *Sandringham Woods*			
	HUCKLE, Clarence William, *Sandringham Farms*			
November	GARDNER, Miss Anne, *Head Coffee Room Maid*	1 Nov 1992		
	WILLIAMS, Eric, *Deputy Head Chauffeur/Photo Printer*	11 Nov 1992		
December	WILLIAMS, Mrs June Irene, *Dairy Maid, Royal Farms, Windsor*	July 1992		
1983				
January	LINES, Richard Clive, *Sandringham Estate Yard*	14 Jan 1993		
July	OSBORNE, Adrian, *Sandringham Estate Yard*	30 July 1993		
September	SENIOR, David Andrew, *Estate Yard Sandringham*			
November	OLIVER, Roger Ian, *Stud Groom, Royal Mews, Windsor*			
December	JONES, Douglas James, *Senior Liveried Helper, Royal Mews*	29 Dec 1993		
1984				
February	MELDRUM, William, *Sandringham Game Department*			
April	BATTERBEE, Malcolm Douglas, *Sandringham Estate Yard*	1 April 1994		
	THORNTON, Jack Greenwood, *Carriage Washer, Royal Mews*			
	HART, John Nelson, *Sandringham Game Department*	13 April 1994		
July	MARWICK, Alexander, *Sturrock, Sandringham Game Department*			

		30 years clasp	40 years clasp	50 years clasp
September	LOWE, Miss Amy, *Daily Help, Clarence House, Queen Elizabeth The Queen Mother's Staff* (*Total of 30 years service 1984. At Marlborough House 1946–53. Clarence House since 1961.*)			
October	ESSON, Edward, *Balmoral Estates*	26 Oct 1994		

1985

April	OATES, Mrs Elsie Avis, *Full time Daily Help, Royal Mews*			
July	NELSON, Cecil John, *Coachman, Royal Mews*	12 July 1995		
September	EVANS, William Robert, *Porter, Industrial Staff, Windsor Castle*			
October	PRENTICE, Miss May, Quail Motion, *Assistant Dresser to The Queen*			
November	FORSYTH, Ronald James, *House Porter Industrial Staff, Windsor Castle*	1 Nov 1995		

1986

January	FITT-SAVAGE, Anthony, *Sandringham*	1 Jan 1996		
	PINE, Robert John, *Sous Chef*	1 Jan 1996		
February	BRAY, Christopher John James, *Page of the Backstairs*	7 Feb 1996		
May	COLLINGS, John, *Head Chauffeur to Queen Elizabeth The Queen Mother*	18 May 1996		
	NORTON, Stephen Joseph, *Balmoral Estates*			
June	DONALD, Peter, *Balmoral*	6 June 1996		
December	MARLOW, Christopher Harry, *Page of the Backstairs*	31 Dec 1996		

1987

February	HODSON, Keith, *Royal Studs*	15 Feb 1997		
April	WHITING, Mrs Margaret Mary, *Cleaner, Royal Mews, Windsor* (*On retirement; broken service; 31 years service.*)			
July	BENEFER, David James, *Sandringham Farms*	31 July 1997		
August	HAWKINS, Richard Charles, *Upholsterer, Superintendent's Staff, Windsor Castle*	21 Aug 1997		

1988

January	MCCARTHY, Donald, *Grieve at the Castle of Mey*	1 Jan 1998		
March	GRIFFIN, David Albert, *Deputy Head Chauffeur*			
May	GODFREY, Clive, *Royal Studs*			
July	BYWORTH, Mrs Gladys, *Daily Help at Clarence House, Queen Elizabeth The Queen Mother's Staff* (*30 years service as a Daily Help.*)			
August	MATTHEWS, Peter Horace, *Sous Chef, 'F' Branch*	1 Aug 1998		
September	SHOWELL, Arthur George, *Head Coachman, Royal Mews* (*Commenced 1 Sept 1968 with Private Horse Scheme, Tile Place Stud. Transferred to Royal Mews Dept. 1 Sept 1969. Continuous Service.*)			
	MATTHEWS, Stephen John, *Rough Rider, Royal Mews*			
November	TAYLOR, Mrs Joan, *Housekeeper, Hampton Court Palace*			
December	JONES, Gwynne, *Sous Chef, 'F' Branch*	21 Dec 1998		

1989

February	NORRIS, Michael Shean, *Royal Studs*	1 Feb 1999		
July	COUTTS, James, *Balmoral Estates*	21 July 1999		
August	OATES, Lawrence Edward George, *Harness Cleaner, Royal Mews*			
December	MUIR, David McNaull, *Head Ponyman, Balmoral Estates*			

		30 years clasp	40 years clasp	50 years clasp

1990

May	THAIN, Norman, *Clerk of Works, Sandringham, later at Balmoral*	4 May 2000
	POOLE, Derek George, *Carriage Washer and Harness Cleaner, Royal Mews; later Courier, Master of the Household's Department*	10 May 2000
	FROHAWK, Ronald Reginald Samuel, *Sandringham Gardens*	
July	WILLIS, Anthony Patrick, *Page of the Presence*	
October	OGILVIE, Alexander, *Head River Ghillie, Balmoral Estates*	
	BOGGIS, Ivan Richard, *Sandringham Farms*	26 Oct 2000
November	MOYES, Mrs Julie Christine, *Housekeeper, Palace of Holyroodhouse*	

1991

March	MASSON, Ian Cooper, *Harvesting Ganger, Forestry Department, Balmoral Estates*
June	NORTHBROOKE-HINE, Miss Susan Bridgett, *Dining Room Assistant*
July	HULLAND, Graham Charles, *Senior Dining Room Assistant*
August	CARTLEDGE, David, *Stallion Man, Royal Stud*
October	MCDONALD, James Alexander, *Painter, Works Department, Balmoral Estates*
November	KERR, John Trodden, *Palace Attendant, Windsor Castle*
December	GRIFFITHS, Keith Howard, *Dining Room Assistant*

1992

March	HURST, Ronald, *Cabinetmaker, Windsor Castle*
April	PICKARD, Miss Elizabeth Ann, *Upholstress*
August	FLOYD, John Henry, *Deputy Page of the Chambers*
November	POTTS, William James, *Game Department, Balmoral*

1993

January	LONG, Mrs Jessie Elizabeth, *Daily Help, Royal Mews, Windsor Castle*
February	WOOD, Miss Marie, *Horsebox Driver, Royal Mews, Windsor Castle*
	POWER, Gerard, *Gilder, Buckingham Palace*
March	MONTEITH, Gordon, *Baile-na-Coille Gardener*
April	MIST, James Thomas George, *Metalsmith, Windsor Castle*
May	CHRISTIAN, Alan, *Reprographic Operator*
	SPRUCE, Norman, *Gardener, Sandringham*
	SIM, William John, *Forester and Farmworker, Balmoral*
	MIDDLETON, David John, *Chief Upholsterer, Buckingham Palace*
June	MASSON, Alan David, *Estate Mechanic, Balmoral*
July	CHAMBERS, Robert John Rogerson, *Senior Liveried Helper, Royal Mews*
August	GOLDSMITH, Norman George, *Palace Attendant, Buckingham Palace*
October	PAXTON, Henry Inglis, *Deputy Head Chauffeur, Royal Mews*
December	COOK, Neil, *Countryside Ranger, Balmoral*
	LEEK, Miss Betty, *Dresser to Queen Elizabeth The Queen Mother*

1994

January	GUERIN, Miss June Marguerite Theresa, *Head Housemaid, Buckingham Palace*
April	WATT, George Duncan, *Stalker, Balmoral Estates*
July	FROHAWK, Stephen Richard, *Sandringham Farms*
August	YOXALL, Kevin Barry, *Palace Foreman, Buckingham Palace*
September	MUTTER, Mrs Betty Winniefrith, *Cloakroom Attendant, Windsor*
October	RUTTY, Anthony Michael, *Sandringham Estate Office*
November	MURPHY, Hugh Joseph Anthony, *Harness Cleaner, Royal Mews*

	30 years clasp	40 years clasp	50 years clasp

1995

February	BARTY, Arthur William Douglas, *Queen Elizabeth The Queen Mother's Household*
March	SUTHERLAND, Sinclair Forbes, *Gardener, Balmoral*
May	STANDEN, Roger Edward, *Foreman, Basement Cleaner, Master of the Household's Department*
June	MELTON, John, *Sandringham Estate*
September	TURVEY, Robert William, *Sandringham*
	STEWART, William Albert, *Palace of Holyroodhouse*
October	BONICI, Tonino, *French Polisher, Master of the Household's Department, Buckingham Palace*
November	ESSON, Hazel Ann, *Balmoral Estates*

1996

January	HAMILTON, Mrs Doris Gay, *Housekeeper, Frogmore House, Master of the Household's Department*
March	WHYBREW, Paul Kevin, *The Queen's Page, Master of the Household's Department*
May	CHONG, Peter, *Gilder*
August	COOK, Phillip Raymond, *Dining Room Assistant, Master of the Household's Department*
September	LANE, Dr Roderick Andrew, *Deputy Head Bookbinder*
October	SMITH, Cecil Raymond, *Sandringham Estate*
	BRADSHAW, David William, *Sandringham Estate*
November	STANDEN, Mrs Molly Winifred Sally, *Daily Help, Master of the Household's Department*
	LOVELL, Barrie Thomas, *Valet to the Duke of Edinburgh*

1997

February	HOLT, Mrs Dora Ann, *Daily Help, Master of the Household's Department, Windsor*
September	MARSHALL, Stephen Henry Ronald, *Assistant Yeoman, Glass pantry*
October	DAY, Joseph Walter Frank, *Helper and Carriage Washer, Royal Mews*
December	RUDD, Henry, *Stud Hand, Royal Stud*
	HARDINGHAM, Anthony John, *Sandringham*

1998

January	EMERY, John Gilbert, *Livery Porter*
February	CROASDALE, Philip Shaun, *Palace Steward*
	HURST, Richard Lee, *Game Department, Sandringham*
	BORER, Richard Royston, *Storeman*
June	CAPSTICK, Ruby Sandra, *Senior Housemaid, Linen Room*
July	SCRIMGEOUR, David Alexander, *Balmoral Estate*
	BANHAM, Keith, *Farm Manager, Sandringham*
August	ROWLANDS, Robert, *Stud Groom, Sandringham*
September	HOLDEN, Phillip Stephen, *Dining Room Assistant*
	RISPIN, Peter, *Stud Hand, Sandringham*
November	BACK, Michael Norman, *Public Access, Sandringham*
	NELSON, Herbert Stanley, *Senior Liveried Helper*
	STANLEY, Brian Alan Ernest, *Stud Groom*
December	BRENT, Anthony Gerald, *Driver and Storekeeper*

1999

April	HAWKES, Andrew, *First Chauffeur*
July	REED, John Leonard, *Stud Hand, Sandringham*
October	KEY, David Edward, *Chauffeur to the Duke of Edinburgh*
	STEWART, Charles John Coulton, *Footman to Queen Elizabeth The Queen Mother*
November	GOODSHIP, Alan William, *Sandringham Estate*

	30 years clasp	40 years clasp	50 years clasp

2000

February	PERRY, Mark Andrew, *Sandringham Estate*
	DENMAN, Adrian John
April	THORNE, David William, *Country Park Ranger, Sandringham*
	MASSON, Lindsey Henderson, *Balmoral Estate*
	JACKSON, Keith, *Gardener, Buckingham Palace*
May	BRYANT, Edna Joan, *Queen Elizabeth the Queen Mother's Household*
	WELBELOVE, Ronald George, MBE RVM, *Queen Elizabeth the Queen Mother's Household*
June	GOLDSMITH, Nigel, *Deputy C. Branch Master of the Household's Dept.*
October	MILLS, Edward Peter, *French polisher Master of the Household's Dept.*

2001

January	GRASSICK, Stephen, *Joiner, Balmoral*
February	WESTWOOD, James, *Accountant, Balmoral*
	RICHARDS, Graham Paul, *Chef, Queen Elizabeth the Queen Mother's Household*

Index

RECIPIENTS OF THE DEVOTED SERVICE MEDAL
THE VICTORIA FAITHFUL SERVICE MEDAL
THE SPECIAL SILVER MEDAL
THE KING GEORGE V LONG AND FAITHFUL SERVICE MEDAL
THE KING GEORGE VI LONG AND FAITHFUL SERVICE MEDAL AND
THE QUEEN ELIZABETH II LONG AND FAITHFUL SERVICE MEDAL

Nicolson, J.F. 68
Niven, John 79
Noon, Miss E. 65
Norman, Ada 84
Norman, H. 66
Norris, Michael Shean 92
Northbrooke-Hine, Miss Susan
  Bridgett 93
Norton, Stephen Joseph 92
Norton, W. 65
Nunn, Arthur Jeffrey 89
Nurse, E. 71
Nurse, Ernest 69
Nurse, George William 78
Nurse, Herbert 75
Nurse, J. 72
Nurse, James 70
Nurse, James Robert 90
Nurse, Mrs Elizabeth 65
Nurse, Ronald Olin 90
O'Dwyer, Miss Mary 89
O'Hagan, Dennis 88
O'Mara, A. 66
Oakes, William 58
Oates, Alfred Francis 89
Oates, David Alfred 90
Oates, Lawrence Edward George 92
Oates, Mrs Elsie Avis 92
Odlum, Mrs Edith 77, 78
Ogilvie, Alexander 93
Oliver, Emily Edith 86
Oliver, Roger Ian 91
Orchard, Francis 51
Osborn, Joseph 63
Osborne, Adrian 91
Osmond, G. 65
Osmond, Owen Thomas 85
Oulton, Charles 83
Overton, Goss 54
Owen, Henry 77
Pace, A.E. 70
Page, Peter Ernest 85
Paice, Stanley A. 83
Painter, Brian Ephriam 89
Painter, Philip Bryan 86
Painter, W. 71
Palmer, J. 71
Panks, Miss Doris Irene 89
Panter, J. 70
Park, Mrs Mary E. 79
Parker, W. 67, 72
Parker, William Henry 70
Parkes, James 83
Parmiter, Wilfred E.B. 84
Parnell, Anthony Vernon 89
Parnell, Horace 64
Parr, Robert 66
Parsons, F.E. 69
Pascoe, Sidney Alfred 75
Patrick, Frederick Owen 85
Pattingale, V.A.E. 71
Paxton, Henry Inglis 93
Payne, George 42
Pearce, E. 67
Pearce, Ernest 84
Pearce, Joseph Matthew 86
Pearce, Mary Anne Whitfield 86
Pearl, James 87
Pearson, George 40
Peel, William 37
Pellet, E.J. 66
Perrins, T. 67

Perry, Michael 90
Petrie, Arthur 87
Phillips, Ernest 64
Phillips, J. 71
Pickard, Miss Elizabeth Ann 93
Picken, Thomas F 77
Pine, Robert John 92
Plevin, H. 68
Pollard, James Leslie 90
Pollard, Thomas 89
Polson, Marion Mackay 80
Ponder, Samuel 54
Poole, Derek George 92
Porter, William Edward 80
Pottinger, G. 69
Pottinger, John 63
Pottow, J. 65
Potts, William James 93
Poupart, P.H. 64
Power, Gerard 93
Power, William 44
Preece, Arthur V. 84
Preece, Norma Ivy Minnie 86
Prentice, G. 66
Prentice, Miss May 92
Preston, John 91
Price, E. J. 66
Price, George 67
Pringle, Arthur 78
Prior, Albert A. 78
Pryor, A. 66
Pugh, E. 66
Pugh, Margaret 70
Purvey, Harold Arthur 88
Puttock, W 65
Quantrill, F.A. 69
Rainbow, E. J. 67
Ralph, A. 71
Ralph, Alfred 67
Ramsdall, W. 65
Rankin, Alexander 59
Ransome, F. 72
Ransome, Frank L. 70
Rapley, J.E. 66
Rawlings, Amelia 69
Rawlings, William 79
Rayment, H. 69
Rayner, Daniel 55
Rayner, Isaac 53
Reed, Frederick J. 76
Reed, Gilbert Frederick 86
Reed, John Leonard 94
Reeves, Minnie 65
Renn, H. 69
Reynolds, T. 65
Richardson, R. 71
Riches, A.J. 71
Riches, Albert Harry 76
Riches, Arthur Robert 75
Riches, G.W. 71
Riches, Geo. W. 69
Riches, H. 71
Riches, James 71
Riches, James John 77
Riches, John 71
Riches, Leonard Horace 85
Riches, P.E. 72
Riches, W.J. 72
Ridgeon, A. 65
Ridgeon, Isaac 56
Ringer, Thomas H. 75
Rispin, Peter 94

Ritchie, Edgar V. 83
Ritchie, John Cecil 91
Rix, Fred 86
Robbins, H. 71
Robbins, Harry 80
Roberts, Archibald 77
Roberts, C. 67
Robertson, Charles 47
Robertson, Ernest 87
Robertson, Jessie 76
Robertson, John Begg 89
Robertson, Margaret 84
Robertson, W. 71
Robertson, William 67
Robinson, Miss Ruby 87
Robinson, Mrs Sylvia Joan 90
Robinson, W. 71
Robinson, William George 56
Roblue, Stanley Wilfred 83
Robson, William 83
Rodda, H.W. 65
Rogers, J. 65
Rose, D. 71
Rose, Margaret 79
Rose, Rizpah 63
Ross, John Grassick 91
Ross, John Walter 90
Ross, Miss Isabel Gettins 86
Ross, William 41
Rous, André 79
Rout, Walter J. 77
Rowlands, Robert 94
Rudd, Henry 94
Ruddle, Arthur 79
Rumsey, William 86
Rush, J. 71
Rutland, Frederick A. 79
Rutty, Anthony Michael 93
Ryan, Miss Hannah 86
Sadd, Richard James 89
Sadler, Ashley John 89
Sanders, F.J. 66
Sands, Thomas 46
Saunders, Elizabeth 78
Saunders, Harry 64
Sawyer, E.J. 69
Sayer, George H. 75
Sayer, J.A. 71
Scallan, Frederick Charles 90
Scott, Edward John 86
Scott, G. 65
Scott, Walter 83
Scrimgeour, David Alexander 94
Seabright, T. 64
Seabrook, William 43
Sealey, Michael Christopher Martin 88
Seaman, Ernest William 90
Seaman, J. 71
Seaman, James 69
Seares, J. 72
Searle, George 33
Sears, John R. 70
Secker, Walter James 87
Senior, David Andrew 91
Senter, J. 71
Senter, John 68
Senter, Walter R. 78
Sergy, Montague 84
Seymour, A.G. 67
Seymour, E.J. 67
Seymour, F. 67
Seymour, John Brown 54

Wells, A.R. 72
Wells, Albert R. 70
Wells, F. 71
Wells, G.E. 71
Wells, George C. 80
Wells, Horace 76
Wells, W. 65
West, John 46
West, S. 66
Whaley, William 48
Wheeler, T. 71
Whincup, David James 87
Whincup, J. 69
Whiting, Frederick F. 84
Whiting, Mrs Margaret Mary 92
Whitwell, Arthur 63
Whybrew, Paul Kevin 94
Wilcock, Reginald 90

Wiles, Albert George 83
Wiles, R. 69
Wilkes, J. 67
Wilkins, Alfred 58
Wilkins, William 50
Williams, Beatrice 77
Williams, Christopher 77
Williams, Eric 91
Williams, Isabella 69
Williams, Mrs June Irene 91
Williams, R.K. 68
Willingham, Clifford L. 80
Willis, Anthony Patrick 93
Wills, Frances 65
Wilson, Archibald 87
Wilson, C. 71
Wilson, Charles 68
Wilson, Douglas W. 79

Wilson, Frederick A. 78
Wilson, G. 67
Wilson, Miss Julia Mary 89
Wilson, Mrs Robina 89
Winkworth, William George 87
Winn, Harriet 65
Wise, David William 88
Wood, E.A. 67
Wood, Herbert Thorpe Warwick 85
Wood, John Kenneth 90
Wood, Miss Marie 93
Woodbridge, A. 65
Woodford, George 51
Woodhouse, H.J. 72
Wood-Murray, Mrs Margaret Johanna 90
Woods, George 58
Woods, William 57

A GROUP OF GEORGE V'S SERVANTS AND SOLDIERS *c.*1912